Cambridge Elements

Elements in Historical Theory and Practice
edited by
Daniel Woolf
Queen's University, Ontario

THINGS OF THE PAST

A Modern Yearning

Kasper Risbjerg Eskildsen
Roskilde University

Shaftesbury Road, Cambridge CB2 8EA, United Kingdom

One Liberty Plaza, 20th Floor, New York, NY 10006, USA

477 Williamstown Road, Port Melbourne, VIC 3207, Australia

314–321, 3rd Floor, Plot 3, Splendor Forum, Jasola District Centre, New Delhi – 110025, India

103 Penang Road, #05–06/07, Visioncrest Commercial, Singapore 238467

Cambridge University Press is part of Cambridge University Press & Assessment, a department of the University of Cambridge.

We share the University's mission to contribute to society through the pursuit of education, learning and research at the highest international levels of excellence.

www.cambridge.org
Information on this title: www.cambridge.org/9781009670890

DOI: 10.1017/9781009342988

© Kasper Risbjerg Eskildsen 2025

This publication is in copyright. Subject to statutory exception and to the provisions of relevant collective licensing agreements, no reproduction of any part may take place without the written permission of Cambridge University Press & Assessment.

When citing this work, please include a reference to the DOI 10.1017/9781009342988

First published 2025

A catalogue record for this publication is available from the British Library

ISBN 978-1-009-67089-0 Hardback
ISBN 978-1-009-34295-7 Paperback
ISSN 2634-8616 (online)
ISSN 2634-8608 (print)

Cambridge University Press & Assessment has no responsibility for the persistence or accuracy of URLs for external or third-party internet websites referred to in this publication and does not guarantee that any content on such websites is, or will remain, accurate or appropriate.

For EU product safety concerns, contact us at Calle de José Abascal, 56, 1°, 28003 Madrid, Spain, or email eugpsr@cambridge.org

Things of the Past

A Modern Yearning

Elements in Historical Theory and Practice

DOI: 10.1017/9781009342988
First published online: October 2025

Kasper Risbjerg Eskildsen
Roskilde University
Author for correspondence: Kasper Risbjerg Eskildsen, eskild@ruc.dk

Abstract: This Element explores the yearning for things of the past, from early modern antiquarianism to the contemporary art market. It tells a global story about scholars who, driven by this yearning, roamed the world and amassed many of its historical artefacts. Their motivation was not just pleasure or profit. They longed for a past that had been lost and strived to reconstruct world history anew. This rewriting of history unleashed heated debates, all over the world and raging for centuries. The debates concerned not only the past but also the present and the future. Many believed that, by revealing a strange and foreign past, the material remains opened a path to modernity. So, the Element investigates not only the history of historical scholarship, and its obsession with things, but also our relationship to the past as modern human beings.

This Element also has a video abstract: www.cambridge.org/EHTP_Eskildsen_abstract

Keywords: global history, historiography, antiquarianism, museums, modernity

© Kasper Risbjerg Eskildsen 2025

ISBNs: 9781009670890 (HB), 9781009342957 (PB), 9781009342988 (OC)
ISSNs: 2634-8616 (online), 2634-8608 (print)

Contents

1 A Modern Yearning   1

2 A History of Things   14

3 Assembling the World   31

4 Dividing the World   45

5 Many Things   62

Bibliography   71

1 A Modern Yearning

1.1 The Guze Kannon

The monks of the Hōryūji Temple protested loudly. For over a thousand years, they had guarded the shrine in the octagonal Hall of Dreams. Hidden behind its walls was the Guze Kannon, a seventh-century bodhisattva (Figure 1). Entering would be sacrilege. Thunder and lightning, the monks warned, might strike intruders, or an earthquake destroy the temple. But the bearded American, Ernest Fenollosa, and his young Japanese companion, Okakura Kakuzō, nonetheless insisted. They worked for the Art Bureau of the Japanese Ministry of Education and were on a mission, exploring temples and shrines in the western region of Japan. The aim was to document and register historical artworks. Now, in the summer of 1884, they had reached the Hōryūji Temple. Over the monks' protests, they made their way into the shrine. Fenollosa later recalled:

> I shall never forget our feelings as the long disused key rattled in the rusty lock. Within the shrine appeared a tall mass closely wrapped about in swathing bands of cotton cloth upon which the dust of ages had gathered. It was no light task to unwrap the contents, some 500 yards of cloth having been used, and our eyes and nostrils were in danger of being choked with the pungent dust. But at last the final folds of the covering fell away, and this marvellous statue, unique in the world, came forth to human sight for the first time in centuries.[1]

The statue was not just exquisite craftsmanship, carved life-size in a single piece of camphor wood and covered in gold, but a witness. It testified immediately, as they unwrapped it. 'We saw at once', Fenollosa remembered, 'that it was the supreme masterpiece of Corean creation, and must have proved a most powerful model to the artists of Suiko', Without the statue, he claimed, scholars 'could only conjecture as to the height reached by the peninsula creations'. Now, the greatness of early Korean art had revealed itself and simultaneously delivered a missing link in the history of Japanese art. The sacrilege had transformed the statue from a sacred object into a thing of the past. To Fenollosa, if not to the monks, it was no longer mediating between the human and the divine, but instead between past and present. The old commitments of religion and tradition had given way to the new and more important commitments of historical scholarship. 'Fortunately', Okakura dryly remarked, 'the thunder did not appear'.[2]

---

[1] Fenollosa, *Epochs*, vol. I, pp. 50–51. Also, Tanaka, *New Times*, pp. 104–8; Storm, 'Excavating'.
[2] Fenollosa, *Epochs*, vol. 1, p. 50. Okakura in Tanaka, *New Times*, p. 106. The statue, scholars later concluded, was probably made in Japan, but inspired by Korean art, Weinstein, 'Yumedono Kannon'.

Figure 1 Seventh-century bodhisattva, Guze Kannon (179 cm), in the Hall of Dreams, where Ernest Fenollosa and Okakura Kakuzō encountered the statue in 1884 and where it remains today. Unknown artist. Photo by Askaen Co. Courtesy The Hōryūji Temple, Japan.

1.2 Knowing Things

This Element is about scholars engaging with and trying to understand the past. It differs from most discussions of historical scholarship. The primary focus is not the printed books and articles that are the outcome of scholarship. Instead, it investigates the process that leads to these works, the encounter between scholars and the material remains of the past. An inspiration has been studies of antiquarianism, traditions of collecting and appreciating old things. In the mid twentieth century, Arnaldo Momigliano showed how modern historical scholarship was indebted to earlier European antiquarianism. In recent decades, Peter N. Miller, Alain Schnapp, and others have not only deepened and expanded Momigliano's investigations but also uncovered different antiquarian traditions in other parts of the world and continuing until today.[3] The Element adds to this research by investigating how the transition from antiquarianism to historical scholarship changed our relationship to the things.

Everywhere and always, the studies of antiquarianism have shown, people have collected old things. In royal courts and sacred sites, such as the Hōryūji Temple, antiquities have affirmed similarities between past and present. Monuments, and other remains, have structured and perpetuated collective memory. They have sustained bonds to ancestors, upheld local and national identity, and confirmed the unchangeable order of society. With the changes of the modern world, the need for such confirmation has only increased, inspiring new attention to conservation, preservation, and material heritage. Many are haunted by nostalgia and dream of a better time before modern disruptions. The world may have lost its way, but the material remains promise the restoration of order. These ways of engaging, however, are possible without scholarly handbooks and museum catalogues, comprehensive registers and surveys, critical footnotes and source editions. The desire for old things existed long before modern historical scholarship and, most likely, would be with us today, even if historical scholarship had never emerged. Heritage and history, as David Lowenthal points out, are not the same.[4]

Historical scholarship enabled another relationship to old things. It transformed them, as Fenollosa and Okakura did with the Guze Kannon, into things of the past. As things of the past, the artefacts were remains of an entirely different world beyond. Historians, philologists, and archaeologists, of course, are human beings and suffer from the same fears and longings as their contemporaries. Many have looked for similarities between past and present, and some have succumbed to nostalgia. But what distinguished historical scholarship from other ways of engaging with old things, and revolutionized our relationship to the past, was the emphasis on differences. The past was not the same as the present, or a better version of the present, but

---

[3] On the methodological approach, Eskildsen, *Modern Historiography*, pp. 1–15. On antiquarianism, Momigliano, 'Ancient History'; Miller, *Momigliano*; Miller, *History*; Schnapp, *conquête*, *World Antiquarianism, histoire universelle*.

[4] Lowenthal, *Heritage Crusade, Past*. Also, on nostalgia and debates about heritage, Becker, *Yesterday*.

foreign and strange.[5] By reconnecting the present with this foreign and strange past, the investigations still had consequences in the world. Historical scholarship was never neutral, or detached from the contemporary world, despite claims to the contrary. However, its peculiar power was the power of anachronism, the baring and bridging of differences in time.

The strangeness emphasized the need for things, making the differences accessible and intelligible. Without, as Fenollosa claimed, people 'could only conjecture'.[6] The remains did not do so by themselves, but in connection and comparison to other artefacts, revealing historical context and development. The Guze Kannon only testified because Fenollosa and Okakura already were familiar with numerous artworks, in Korea and Japan as well as in the rest of the world. Historical scholarship hereby both intensified and diversified antiquarian interests. Even remains with no relation to the present, and no nostalgic appeal, became cherished as pieces in the puzzle of the past. Artefacts that did not belong to one's family, city, nation, or religion still mattered as historical sources. By the end of the nineteenth century, when Fenollosa and Okakura arrived at the Hōryūji Temple, the yearning for things of the past had become all-consuming. Scholars were searching for remains everywhere, even if it demanded the violation of sacred shrines and the disruption of traditions that they once preserved.

For many, including Okakura as explained later, disruption was the purpose. Their work, deciphering ancient writings and forgotten languages, exploring ruins and muddy archaeological sites, and arguing with angry monks in distant temples, was a service to modernity. The past was important because it unsettled, rather than confirmed, collective memories and shared values and believes. By uncovering its strangeness, historical scholarship proved that the present was only a passing moment in time, that contemporary habits and convictions were not eternal, and that other ways of living and thinking were possible. It revealed that the order of society was not unchangeable. So, the approach was not just different from other ways of engaging with old things, but a refutation. Historical scholarship disproved continuities, denied similarities, and, consequently, accelerated the changes of the modern world.

1.3 Debating Things

The yearning for things of the past not only prompted scholars to search for remains, but also to amass artefacts from around the world in museums, primarily in Europe and North America. These efforts remain controversial.

---

[5] For some recent discussions, Lorenz, *Breaking up*. On the early modern origins, Fasolt, *Limits*. On the connection to modern conceptions of time, Phillips, *Historical Distance*; Hartog, *Régimes*; Fritzsche, *Stranded*; Koselleck, *Vergangener Zukunft*.

[6] Fenollosa, *Epochs*, p. 50.

Debates about acquisition and restitution, the return of artefacts to their places of origin, continue to divide the museum community today. This Element only mentions some of the many controversies in passing. The reader should look elsewhere for more thorough treatments of, say, the British Royal Marines' looting of the ancient African Kingdom of Benin in 1897 or discussions about the return of the so-called Elgin marbles from the British Museum to the Parthenon in Athens.[7] The Element instead explores how and why scholars, all over the world, developed an obsession with material remains. This exploration may help explain some of the passions and persuasions of the contemporary debates.

In the museum debates, a central distinction has been between 'universalist' and 'nationalist' approaches to the ownership and preservation of artefacts. From a 'universalist' viewpoint, material remains belong to all humankind. They have been traded and exchanged over borders for centuries and originated in cultures and countries that no longer exist. Why should a contemporary Muslim Egyptian have any special claims to the great monuments of the Pharaohs, who spoke a different language and believed in different Gods? From a 'nationalist' viewpoint, modern collections represent earlier injustices and inequalities. The continued trade with antiquities promotes looting and the destruction of archaeological sites and further contributes to the unequal distribution of artefacts across the world. What entitles a few museums in Europe and North America to so many of the world's historical artefacts?[8] The distinction between 'universalist' and 'nationalist' approaches is based upon twentieth-century cultural property laws and rooted in the belief that old things are things of the past. Both positions assume that material remains reveal the past, that the past is relevant to the contemporary world, and that the artefacts therefore must be preserved and exhibited. There are, of course, other arguments for and against restitution. Some want to restore and revive traditions. All over the world, people are now obsessed with heritage and haunted by nostalgia. Others worry about the standards of care, and level of appreciation, in 'source' countries. However, historical scholarship helped frame the debates.

The Element explores how the discussions developed over time, together with the development of historical scholarship. Section 2 shows how the encounter with people in other parts of the world, and their material remains, challenged Europeans to reconsider their views of world history. This, as described in Section 3, prompted the need for 'universal' or 'encyclopaedic'

---

[7] On Benin, Phillips, *Loot.* On the Elgin marbles, Robertson, *Who Owns.* For arguments for restitution, Sarr and Savoy, *Restituer*; D. Hicks, *Brutish Museums.* For different perspectives, Jacobs, *Plunder?*; Grau, *Under discussion*; Cuno, *Whose Culture, Who Owns.*

[8] Merryman, 'Two Ways'; Cuno, *Who Owns.*

museums, with artefacts from all over the world. The museums also inspired scholars outside of Europe to reconsider the artefacts that remained. These scholars were not necessarily 'nationalists', in the sense of the current museum debates. However, most were convinced of the benefits of historical scholarship and therefore wanted to preserve some artefacts in local museums. Section 4 shows how these convictions in the mid twentieth century inspired early debates about acquisition and restitution. Finally, Sections 1 and 5 explore connections between the global engagement with material remains and visions of modernity. So, the Element is not intended as an intervention into the museum debates, but as an investigation of ideas and practices, informing everyone. This investigation reveals not only downsides of historical scholarship, and its obsession with things, but also why it mattered.

1.4 Exhibiting the Past

An acute observer of the European relationship to things was the Japanese scholar Kume Kunitake, who between 1871 and 1873 travelled across North America and Europe with a government delegation. The mission was part of a larger effort to modernize the country. For more than two centuries the Tokugawa Shogunate had partly isolated Japan from the surrounding world. In 1853, the American navy forced the country to open its ports. After a period of unrest, the Meiji Restoration of 1868 not only reinstated imperial power, but also started a process of rapid reform. The delegation, which included several high government officials, should prepare these reforms and document what it meant to be modern. Kume served as clerk and record keeper.

In Europe, Kume was especially fascinated by the many large institutions – archives, libraries, and museums – dedicated to preserving, exploring, and exhibiting the past. The delegation visited several such institutions, and he repeatedly commented on the oddity. In the library of the British Museum, he noted that some of the books 'have bloodstains on them; some have been retrieved from the embers of fires. Even remnants of incomplete and damaged books have been collected and are kept in glass cases'. In the crammed galleries on the first floor, he saw British pottery and bronze artefacts, Scandinavian prehistoric stone tools, and many Egyptian objects, including 'ancient coffins and mummies four thousand years old' (Figure 2). Some objects, he remarked, had been 'excavated from the earth', but European archaeologists 'admire and value all such objects and will not discard any of them'. Later, at the museum of the French National Library, he remarked that while the Japanese hurried to 'throw out the old and bring in the new', Europeans were 'slow to discard old artefacts'.[9]

---

[9] Kume, *Iwakura Embassy*, vol. II, pp. 108–9, vol. III, p. 59.

Figure 2 The First Egyptian Room on the first floor the British Museum, as it looked when Kume Kunitake visited. Photo by Frederick York, 1875. Courtesy The Trustees of the British Museum, United Kingdom.

Kume's comments may seem unjust to his countrymen. Japan possessed many great collections of historical artefacts, some, like at the Hōryūji Temple, older and larger than most of those found in Europe. Since the Middle Ages, Japanese writers and artists had celebrated the aesthetic qualities of the worn and the aged. During the eighteenth and nineteenth centuries, a strong antiquarian culture had emerged with private gatherings, exhibits, and societies.[10] Revering old things was not strange to the Japanese.

The European relationship to the things, nonetheless, seemed to differ in significant ways. Museums did not just store artefacts that were valuable or beautiful or carried symbolic or religious significance, but, as Kume noted, almost everything surviving. The purpose was not primarily to admire or worship the artefacts, but to make the past available to contemporaries. They were presented together with other remains from the same period and place, allowing for an understanding of historical context, and in chronological series, offering an overview of historical developments. The museums, by bringing things together in space, allowed for travels through time. Going through the

---

[10] Suzuki, *Antiquarians*.

galleries of the British Museum (Figure 3), Kume reported, 'the sequence of stages of civilization . . . are immediately apparent to the eye'.[11] The collections, moreover, were open to the public. They not just benefitted individual collectors, religious institutions, or royal households but presented the past to society at large.

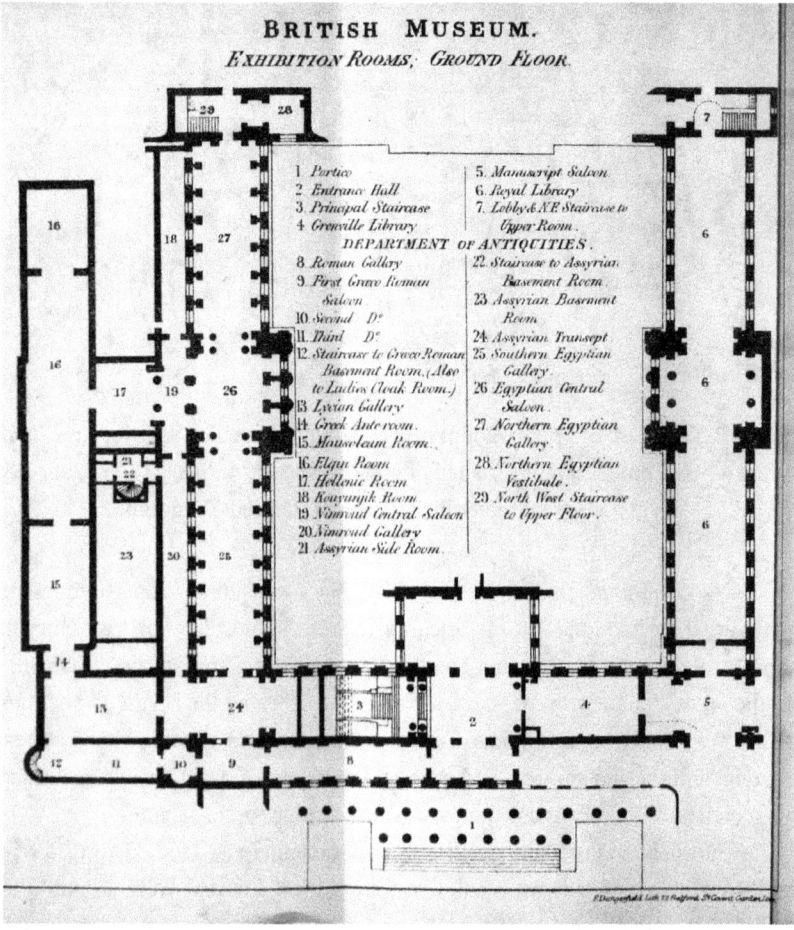

Figure 3 Plan of the galleries of the Department of Antiquities on the ground floor of the British Museum that Kume Kunitake walked through, following the 'stages of civilization'. *A Guide to the Exhibition Rooms of the Departments of Natural History and Antiquities* (London: Printed by order of the Trustees, 1871), p. v. Courtesy Biodiversity Heritage Library, United States of America.

---

[11] Kume, *Iwakura Embassy*, vol. II, p. 109.

1.5 A Recent Yearning

This obsession with reviving and exhibiting the past was recent. After visiting the South Kensington Museum, later the Victoria and Albert Museum, Kume remarked that it 'had not been very long established'.[12] He continued to admonish his Japanese readers not to overestimate the antiquity of European institutions. Only during last forty years, he claimed, European countries had developed into their current shape. At the beginning of the century, great industrial cities like Liverpool and Glasgow had fewer than a hundred thousand inhabitants. Trade only boomed with the introduction of steamships and railways. Many great fortunes had been created in the last decades. The same could be said for historical museums. Like the Japanese, Europeans had always collected and many of the objects in contemporary museums came from these collections. However, only recently large public museums had been created, or reorganized, with the specific purpose of reviving and exhibiting the past.

Few of the museums that Kume visited were older than the industrial towns of Northern England and Scotland. The British Museum, often considered the oldest such museum in the world, was established in 1753 and opened to the public in 1759. However, the institution was not initially a historical museum, but primarily a collection of books, manuscripts, and specimens of natural history, from the eclectic private collection of the physician Sir Hans Sloane. The museum subsequently amassed more historical artefacts and established an independent Department of Antiquities in 1807. During the first half of the nineteenth century, the museum rapidly expanded its collection, partly thanks to British wars and colonial conquests. Its large collection of Egyptian antiquities was established after the defeat of Napoleon's army in 1801 at Alexandria, where the British captured many boxes filled with statues and other antiquities, ready to be shipped to Paris. Others were acquired by traders, diplomats, and private collectors. A British diplomat to Constantinople, Thomas Bruce, 7th Earl of Elgin, dismantled the marbles from the Parthenon in Athens and sold them to the British government in 1816.[13]

At first, curators at the British Museum disagreed whether they should organize the many new acquisitions according to aesthetic or historical principles. Only gradually the many antiquities were placed in historical context and chronological series.[14] The engagement with the past, moreover, was an ongoing process, demanding constant reordering. Still in 1852, the Hungarian exile politician and polymath Frenec Pulszky critically observed about the British Museum:

---

[12] Ibid., p. 57. [13] Miller, *Noble Cabinet*. [14] Jenkins, *Archaeologists*.

> We go from the masterworks of the Parthenon straight up to the stuffed seal and buffalo; and two monster giraffes stand as sentinels before the gallery of vases. Moreover, in the arrangement of the several works of art, we see no leading idea, no system carried out continuously. The only arrangement approaching to a system is a geographical one, where we find monuments of the same country placed together, but without any regard to chronology or style. The colossal figures of the Pharaohs are mixed with Greek works of the Ptolomies, the monuments of the era of Hadrian with those of the time of Pericles.[15]

Pulszky instead praised the Glyptothek in Munich and the Royal Museum in Berlin. Both these museums had opened their doors to the public in 1830. Ludwig I, who became King of Bavaria in 1825, acquired most of the objects for the Glyptothek during the first decades of the nineteenth century. The museum was from the beginning organized in a chronological series, from Egypt to Rome, and ending with modern sculptors, such as Antonio Canova and Bertel Thorvaldsen, considered worthy inheritors of the classical tradition. The Royal Museum in Berlin started with a small older collection, donated by the Hohenzollen royal family, and only gradually expanded. The classical archaeologist Eduard Gerhard, who was hired in 1833, reorganized the museum in historical order, with new Etruscan and Greek cabinets, opening in 1844 and 1858.[16] Egyptian antiquities, previously housed in the Monbijou castle, were added with the so-called New Museum, constructed between 1843 and 1855.

The work with the Egyptian collections demanded not only new buildings, but also an expedition to Egypt, travelling as far as the Sudan and the Sinai Peninsula, between 1842 and 1845, and returning with 15,000 antiquities and plaster casts. In 1846, the Prussian ministers of finance and culture triumphantly reported to King Friedrich Wilhelm IV that his new Egyptian museum would surpass other similar museums and 'have the advantage, for the first time, to be established from an art historical point of view'. The expedition, they explained, 'always was careful to include characteristic pieces from all dynasties until the time of the Ptolemies and the Roman Emperors in the collection'. Similar changes happened in other parts of the Europe. By 1872, when the Japanese delegation arrived, the continent was full of museums, exhibiting the history of art. To the visitors, these museums appeared yet another aspect of modernity that needed to be learned. 'At the root of the march of progress in the West', Kume concluded, 'is a profound love of antiquity'.[17]

---

[15] Pulszky, 'Progress', pp.11–12.
[16] Vierneisel, *Glypthothek München*; Fendt, 'Antikeverständnis'. For context, Paul, *First Modern Museums*; Pomian, *musée*, vol. II.
[17] Messling, 'Ägyptische Abteilung', p. 78; Kume, *Iwakura Embassy*, vol. III, p. 60. Also, on the expedition to Egypt, Marchand, *German Orientalism*, pp. 89–90.

The transformation happened soon after in Japan. During the 1870s and 1880s, the rich culture of Japanese antiquarianism experienced a profound crisis. Older Chinese systems of learning were replaced by new European ones. Japanese antiquaries trained in classical traditions were removed from central positions. The University of Tokyo, founded in 1877, hired professors, who understood and identified with modern historical thinking. Fenollosa was invited already in 1878. Kume became professor of history in 1888. Edward Morse, the first professor of zoology, who also was a passionate collector and frequented Japanese antiquarian circles, noted the different approaches to objects. Until recently, Japanese antiquaries were not only less specialized, but also, he wrote in his diary, 'never so systematic or scientific and generally not so curious nor so exact as to the age and locality of the objects'. This now changed. In the following decades, Japanese collections were reorganized as well. The authorities registered and gathered objects from around the country, culminating with the opening of the Imperial Museums in Tokyo, Nara, and Kyoto in 1889, 1895, and 1897. Fenollosa's and Okakura's visit to the Hōryūji Temple, in the summer of 1884, was a part of these efforts.[18]

1.6 Art and Industry

Kume's arguments for the connection between history and modernity were utilitarian. Manufacture, he claimed, depended upon historical museums. They were resources for artistic education and industrial innovation, and therefore sources of progress. These arguments were echoed in other contemporary Japanese reports about European museums and mirrored the policies of the Meiji government. They also reflected contemporary ideas in Europe. In Prussia, artistic education, mercantile interests, and the competition over industrial development served as justification for the establishment of an art museum. The South Kensington Museum, which prompted Kume's reflections about the newness of European progress, was established in 1852 after the first World's Fair, the Great Exhibition of the Works of Industry of All Nations, and its original name was Museum of Manufactures. It consciously combined the history of art with the history of craftsmanship to inspire contemporary designers.[19]

---

[18] Morse, *Japan*, vol. II, pp. 106–7. On antiquarianism and its crisis, Suzuki, *Antiquarians*. On changing views of history, Tanaka, *Japan's Orient, New Times*. On museums, Tseng, *Imperial Museums*.

[19] On Japanese policies, Tseng, *Imperial Museums,* pp. 18–38. On Prussia, Weitmann, *Klassische Antike*, pp. 11–15. On South Kensington Museum, Bryant, *Art and Design*. The museum changed name to Museum of Ornamental Art in 1853, to South Kensington Museum in 1857, and to Victoria and Albert Museum in 1899. Plessen, 'Art and Design', p. 11.

These utilitarian arguments, however, do not explain the obsessive collecting of historical artefacts. The use of museums for education and innovation justified displaying exquisite works of art and craftsmanship. Placing these works together with other inferior objects made less sense. To many, the historical agglomeration only undermined their function. It diverted attention and resources away from the works of art most worthy of imitation. It served a scholarly purpose, foreign to the arts. In 1833, Wilhelm von Humboldt, as government supervisor of the Royal Museum in Berlin, argued against the inclusion of Egyptian antiquities, Slavic and Germanic prehistoric remains, and ethnographic objects into the museum. 'The purpose of the museum', he protested, 'is obviously promoting art, propagating the taste for it, and ensuring its enjoyment'. It should contain objects that could be adored immediately and, in Humboldt's words, 'free of all scholarship'. The proposed additions had little artistic value. The artefacts were too complicated and too diverse to understand and only of 'historical significance', and therefore did not belong in the museum. As late as 1857, the head of the British Museum, Antonio Panizzi, similarly argued that the galleries should be reserved for classical art. The rooms occupied 'by what is called British and Irish antiquities and by the ethnographic collection, might then be turned to better account. It does not seem right that such valuable space should be taken up by Esquimaux dresses, canoes and hideous feather idols, broken flints and so on'.[20]

1.7 The Past in the Present

Okakura offered a different explanation for the connection between history and modernity, especially in *The Ideals of the East* and *The Awakening of Japan*, published in 1903 and 1904. In these books, which were written in English, Okakura reflected on the transformation of Japan over the last century. The study of ancient artefacts had been central to process. The Tokugawa Shogunate had not just isolated Japan from the rest of the world, but also, he claimed, petrified society in an unchangeable order. Material remains proved that Japanese society once had been organized in other ways. Okakura was careful not to give all the credit to modern historical scholarship. In recent decades, Japanese scholars might have learned 'more systematic methods', but their 'Renaissance' emerged out of older traditions. It was the antiquaries who first had introduced the Japanese to their past. However, when modern scholars 'ransacked the monasteries throughout the whole extent of the empire', they contributed to this renewal.[21]

---

[20] Humboldt, *Gesammelte Schriften*, vol. XII.2, pp. 573–74. Also, Weitmann, *Klassische Antike*, pp. 41–68; Panizzi in Miller, *Noble Cabinet*, pp. 191–92.
[21] Okakura, *Awakening*, pp. 192–3. Also, for context, Weston, *Japanese Painting*, pp. 218–66, and, for a different reading, Tanaka, *New Times*, pp. 106–10, 128–33.

Okakura's and Fenollosa's ransacking of the Hōryūji Temple, and discovery of the Guze Kannon, was an example. The statue embodied, he explained, the idealism of a distant age when Buddhism was first introduced to Japan. It showed 'a spirit of intense refinement and purity, such as only great religious feeling could have produced' and revealed ideas of 'divinity, in this early phase of national realisation'. Japan had been shaped by different influences from across Asia, and an imported religion, Buddhism, played a key role in the formation of the nation. These different influences were documented in its large and untouched collections of antiquities. The whole country had become 'a museum of Asian civilization' where 'the historic wealth of Asiatic culture can be consecutively studied through its treasured specimens'.[22]

This exploration of the differences of the Japanese past not only served a scholarly purpose. Historical scholarship emphasized the distinction between past and present. At the same time, through the things, it reconnected past and present. This new connection to a foreign and strange world allowed contemporaries to reimagine themselves. Once revealed, the antiquities proved to the Japanese that it was possible at once to develop, learn from others, and remain true to oneself. So, the 'downfall of the sanctity of Buddhist monasteries' opened for a new beginning.[23] The violation of the shrine in the Hall of Dreams transformed not only the Guze Kannon from a sacred object into a thing of the past but also society at large. Behind the rusty lock of the shrine, if we can believe Okakura, modern Japan was waiting.

This modernizing effect does not depend upon the context of Meiji Japan. It is an effect of historical scholarship, which has transformed societies all over the world and continues transforming them today. Japan was only the latest frontier and other countries followed. The effect also contributed to the modern yearning for things of the past. Scholars both wanted to know the past and believed that their investigations mattered in the present. The yearning was fuelled by a longing for a world that had been lost as well as by hopes for change. Both impulses rested upon the conviction, established long before Okakura, that the only reliable way to know the past was through things. The next section investigates how European scholars arrived at this conviction. It also shows how they banished much of the world from history, and, consequently, unleased a global debate about who belonged in the new world history of things.

---

[22] Okakura, *Ideals*, pp. 103, 6–7.   [23] Ibid., p. 225.

2 A History of Things

2.1 The Ruins of Palenque

In March 1786, Captain Antonio del Río was ordered to travel into the rainforest of Chiapas, at the border between the Captaincy General of Guatemala and Viceroyalty of New Spain, to investigate the ruins of an ancient city, near the town of Palenque. The ruins had been explored before, but his superiors wanted additional information. When del Río arrived, the site was overgrown. Doors and windows had been blocked with stones. The captain was no scholar, but he had received instructions beforehand and knew what he was looking for. He went to work with determination and local Amerindians were ordered to help. They cleared the vegetation and, with iron bars and pickaxes, forced all doors and windows open. The buildings were measured and the underground excavated. The former inhabitants, del Río concluded, resembled those of the nearby Yucatan Peninsula.[24] They belonged, as we now know, to the ancient Mayan civilization of Central America.

Del Río's conjectures did not end there. He also proposed that Romans, Greeks, or Phoenicians may have visited the city and stayed for a period. Such speculations about Old and New World connections had been going on for centuries. However, the captain's approach to the question was new. Unlike most early modern writers, he did not refer to biblical passages or ancient writings to support his theories. He also made a clear distinction between the contemporary people of Chiapas and those of the Mayan city. The captain investigated a past that did not resemble the present. This past, because it was foreign and strange, was only available through the remains. His conclusions about the resemblance to Yucatan were based on, in del Río's words, 'monuments spared by the passing of the centuries'. His conjectures about Old World visitors were derived from artwork in the buildings. His many excavations across the site were 'indispensable', he claimed, 'to form some idea of the first inhabitants'. With his report to Madrid, he included not only illustrations, but also material artefacts, among these a seventh-century stela later identified as belonging to the throne of King Pakal, documenting the 'degree' of development of 'the ancients of the country' (Figure 4).[25]

Del Río's report reflected a larger shift in how scholars approached the past. During the previous centuries, traditional history writing had lost credibility. Critics and sceptics questioned authors, who once had been beyond reproach, and challenged the great biblical and mythical narratives that framed world

---

[24] Del Río's report in Cabello Carro, *Política*, pp. 130–47. Also, for context, Cañizares-Esguerra, *How to Write*, pp. 321–45.
[25] Cabello Carro, *Política*, pp. 135, 131, 140.

Figure 4 Seventh-century limestone stela (46.5 x 29.5 cm) from the throne of King Pakal in Palenque, collected by Antonio del Río and sent to Madrid in 1787. Unknown artist. Courtesy Museo de América, Spain.

history. During the eighteenth century, many still referred to and believed in these narratives, but they no longer could be taken for granted. Consequently, large parts of the human past, especially the earliest periods, appeared unknowable without additional sources. Scholars, either longing for confirmation or hoping for alternatives, turned to material remains. They strived to reconstruct history anew from surviving monuments and artefacts. Del Río's mission to Palenque was an ambitious attempt, closely supervised by authorities in Madrid and Guatemala City, to insert the Americas into this new world history of the things.

2.2 Sons of Noah

When Europeans first arrived in the Americas, they did not need ancient monuments and artefacts to frame their history. Most European scholars simply assumed that the inhabitants of New World, somehow, belonged within biblical history. The problem was not the Bible, but rather how these newfound people fitted in. God had created the world around 4,000 years before the birth of Christ. All people on earth descended from Adam and Eve, and, after the Deluge, Noah and one of his three sons, Japhet, Shem, and Ham. All human beings were members of the same family, and their history interconnected. An open question was how and when the Amerindians had arrived in the New World. Noah's Ark came to rest on Mount Ararat, in Armenia, so they must have crossed either the Pacific or the Atlantic Ocean. The Spanish soldier and historian Gonzalo Fernández de Oviedo in 1535 suggested that their ancestors were Carthaginians or, more likely, Spaniards, who settled during the reign of the mythical King Héspero. Francisco López de Gómara, the secretary of Hernán Cortés who defeated the Aztec Empire in 1521, proposed that the Amerindians descended from the sunken continent of Atlantis. Others guessed that Ulysses had travelled there after the Trojan war, that Noah's grandson, Canaan, may have gone after being cursed for his father's sin, or that the Amerindians were the people of Ophir, from whom King Solomon had received a shipment of gold, precious stones, and algum wood. Many discussed whether they descended from the ten lost tribes of Israel, who were captured by the Assyrian King Shalmaneser and disappeared afterwards. These different theories were in 1607 summarized by Gregorio García in *Origin of the Indians of the New World*, which became a bestseller across Europe and inspired many other ideas.[26]

The stories about the Amerindians were not very different from the stories that Europeans told about themselves. Many Europeans claimed to descend from Trojans, who had survived the destruction of their city. The Spanish

---

[26] Huddleston, *Origins*; Grafton, *New Worlds*; Gliozzi, *Adam*.

wanted older roots as descendants of Tubal, the grandson of Noah. The Holy Roman Empire, a polyglot conglomerate of states and cities that held together much of Europe, was interpreted as the last of the four world monarchies, which had been prophesied in the Book of Daniel. The Holy Roman Empire was the direct continuation of Roman Empire and the embodiment of universal Christendom. After his election as Emperor in 1519, Charles V of Spain claimed to be the rightful inheritor. A later court historiographer, Florián de Ocampo, argued that King Héspero also had ruled over Italy and that the Spanish had founded the city of Rome.[27] These stories sustained and justified a religious and political order. Explaining the New World within the framework was a way to expand this order. With colonization, the Amerindians simply returned to the place where they always had belonged.

2.3 Before Adam

For those who wanted to challenge the political and religious order, the encounter with other people around the world also offered an opportunity. With European expansion, the limits of the biblical history became increasingly apparent. While astronomers, from Copernicus to Galileo, challenged the Bible's geocentric universe, other scholars questioned its Mediterranean-centred account of the past. The world, historians pointed out, had seen more than just four large monarchies. Missionaries reported back that Chinese history was very old, starting before the Deluge. Similar ancient chronologies, philologists revealed, existed for the Egyptians, Scythians, and Chaldeans. Many ignored these findings or discarded them as irrelevant or too insecure. Some attempted to reinterpret divergent evidence within the biblical framework. Noah may have travelled east, and early Chinese history was just a perverted memory. The early Chinese emperors were biblical patriarchs, but with different names. The time between creation and the universal flood may have been shorter, if calculated differently, allowing for a longer range of history. Others, however, started arguing that the biblical account of world history should be reconsidered.[28]

One important sceptic was the French scholar Isaac La Peyrère. In two treatises, published in 1655, he questioned the biblical tradition on several levels. La Peyrère's central claim was that the inhabitants of the Americas, China, and other parts of the world did not descend from Adam but had been created earlier. They were pre-Adamites. The Deluge was only a local event and

---

[27] Burke, 'History'; Völkel, 'German Historical Writing'; Ostenfeld-Suske, 'Writing Official History'. On Héspero and Rome, Erasmus, *Origins*, pp. 49–51.

[28] Rossi, *Dark Abyss*. On the political challenge of history, Fasolt, *Limits*. On the four monarchies, Grafton, *What Was History*, pp. 167–73. On China and world history, Kley, 'Europe's "Discovery"'.

had not eradicated all people on earth. La Peyrère's theory solved contradictions within the Bible and explained older chronologies and the encounter with people, who were not discussed in the Bible. However, his reading was no longer literal. The Old Testament appeared as a historical document, only relevant to the history of the early Israelites, and not a history of the world. The treatises provoked controversy, and, like Galileo, La Peyrère was forced to retract his ideas. Nonetheless, the historical nature of the Bible was soon confirmed in other works, most prominently Benedict Spinoza's notorious *Historical-Political Treatise* and Ricard Simon's careful philological work, *Critical History of the Old Testament,* published in 1670 and 1678.[29]

2.4 After Myth

As early as the sixteenth century, some scholars also questioned other European origin stories, the supposed pedigree of princes and nations among mythical kings and exiled Trojans. Some found inspiration in ancient scepticism, and the approach became known as 'historical Pyrrhonism', after the ancient sceptic philosopher Pyrrho of Elis. Nothing about the past, the sceptics claimed, could be known with certainty. The sources were often not contemporary. Even those that reported about their own time only offered partisan and partial viewpoints. The discussions culminated in the 1720s, when the French Royal Academy of Inscriptions and Belles-Lettres engaged in a heated debate about the knowability of the beginnings of history. Many of the sources to Roman history disappeared when the Gauls burnt and sacked the city in 390 BC. The earliest history, moreover, was full of fables, which even had been questioned by ancient historians. Much seemed to have been copied from Greek sources, which were no more reliable. A similar critique was launched against the sources to the earliest Chinese history. These sources also contained fables and could not immediately be believed. Most Chinese books had been burned in 213 BC.[30] So, the problem may not just be whether people existed before Adam, but also to account for the many years before the first reliable written sources. Even if one accepted Moses' testimony, as most scholars did, much of human history remained in darkness. In his *Letters on the Study and Use of History*, written during the 1730s, Lord Bolingbroke concluded:

---

[29] Popkin, *Isaac La Peyrère*. For context, Gliozzi, *Adam*, pp. 243–90, 427–86. On biblical criticism, Scholder, *Ursprünge*, and, on the historicization of the Bible in the eighteenth century, Sheehan, *Enlightenment Bible*.

[30] On early critique, Burke, *Renaissance Sense*, pp. 69–76. On historical Pyrrhonism, Scheele, *Wissen*; Matytsin, *Specter*, pp. 239–46. On theories of beginnings, Zedelmaier, *Anfang*. On China, Kley, 'Europe's "Discovery"', pp. 373–74, 377–80.

The nature of man, and the constant course of human affairs, render it impossible that the first ages of any nation which forms itself, should afford authentic materials for history. We have none such concerning the originals of any of those nations that actually subsist. Shall we expect to find them concerning nations dispersed, or extinguished, two or three thousand years ago?[31]

The problem seemed even more pressing for the Americas. The Romans and Chinese had left a rich written record, covering thousands of years and recognizable to Europeans as history writings. Amerindians did not appear to have anything similar. Mesoamericans had pictorial writings, and the Incas represented their past in pictures as well as in quipus, knotted strings containing information about genealogies and historical events. Many European scholars, however, questioned the reliability of Amerindian sources and the ability of non-alphabetical writings to convey accurate information. This critique only increased with the sceptical discussions about the knowability of the past.[32]

If Herodotus, Livy, or Confucius could not be trusted, why believe an anonymous pictorial representation of the Incan past? If the classical origin myths of European people should be discarded, why keep Amerindian stories, where fable and history were equally closely intertwined? As early as 1688, the English scholar Paul Rycaut, dismissed histories based on Amerindian sources and oral traditions. The early history of European nations was unknown, so, he argued, it would be irrational to expect that 'these illiterate Creatures' should know anything about 'those Ages; of which the learned parts of the World acknowledge their ignorance, and confess themselves to be in the dark even as to those matters which concern their own histories'.[33]

This sceptical critique of ancient historians and myths was also turned into a defence of the Bible. The Italian philosopher of history, Giambattista Vico made a sharp distinction between Jewish tradition, recording events as they happened, and later mythical histories of other people. Myths were important sources, revealing the parallel development of nations. Amerindians, Vico proposed, resembled ancient Germans. However, for the earliest periods, only the Bible provided secure knowledge and delivered a framework for historical interpretation. Throughout the eighteenth century, historians continued speculating whether their nations descended from one or another grandson of Noah. Most insisted that world history only had lasted around 6,000 years, starting with Adam and Eve in the Garden of Eden. Even if much of world history

---

[31] Bolingbroke, *Letters*, p. 59.
[32] Boone, 'Mesoamerican History'; Rabasa, 'Alphabetical Writing'; Julien, 'Inca Historical Forms'. Also, on scepticism, Cañizares-Esguerra, *How to Write*, pp. 60–129.
[33] Rycaut, 'Translator', unpag.

appeared uncertain, and the edifice of biblical history crumbled from within, the outer scaffolds remained.[34]

2.5 A Roman History of Things

Many scholars pointed to material remains as a possible solution to the question about the knowability of the past. If most histories were only copies of copies, and full of lies, fables, and conjectures, remnants of the past had survived. For recent history, scholars emphasized the reliability of legal and official documents. These were the outcomes of peace negotiations, dictates of the princes, and court cases, and offered unquestionable evidence about the events. In the Holy Roman Empire, which had survived for almost a thousand years, even medieval documents remained part of the existing legal order and were carefully stored and preserved in princely archives. The archival obsession of the modern historical discipline is largely the outcome of this early modern recourse to legal and official documents.[35]

Other scholars, especially when discussing early history, instead turned to monuments and artefacts. This interest in antiquities relied upon the tradition of antiquarianism. After the fall of the Roman Empire, classical art and architecture remained a part of European tradition. Materials were reused, imitated, and inspired repeated revivals. From the fifteenth century, Italian humanists started systemically investigating the ancient city of Rome through its remains. Princes and scholars gathered antiquities and exhibited them in their cabinets. From 1471, the popes displayed their ancient bronze sculptures at the Capitol in Rome and, a few decades later, their marbles, including the recently unearthed Apollo and Laocoön statues, in the Belvedere Court of the Vatican Palace. Those passionate about the disappearing world of antiquity became known as antiquaries.[36]

Monuments and artefacts, some antiquaries insisted, were not only beautiful, but also opened a door to the past. Some were valuable as historical sources. Coins revealed much about names, places, and historical events, which had not been preserved in history books. Engraved gemstones delivered insights into ancient mythology and beliefs, heroes and legends, customs and manners. However, even without historical scholarship, the material remains offered an

---

[34] On Vico, Rossi, *Dark Abyss*, pp. 168–82. Also, on Vico and America, Kubler, 'Vico's Idea'; Cañizares-Esguerra, *How to Write*, pp. 103–5. On biblical narratives in Britain, Kidd, *British Identities*, pp. 9–72, and in Scandinavia, Evju, *Ancient Constitution*, pp. 97–105. Also, on the eighteenth-century debates, Pocock, *Barbarism*; Sheehan, *Enlightenment Bible*.
[35] Eskildsen, *Modern Historiography*, esp. pp. 47–56, 75–105, Friedrich, *Geburt*.
[36] On antiquarianism, Momigliano, 'Ancient History'; Weiss, *Renaissance Discovery*; Schwab, *Art*. On collections, Pomian *musée*, vol. I.

immediate, tangible, and emotional connection to antiquity. 'Antiquaries', the former Oxford professor Meric Casaubon observed in 1638, revered antiquities 'because those visible superviving evidences of antiquitie represent unto their minds former times, with as strong an impression, as if they were actually present, and in sight as it were'.[37]

The antiquities could be interpreted in ways that supported biblical and mythical history, but they also offered alternatives. During the eighteenth century, European scholars proposed new histories of antiquity, from the Egyptians to the Roman Empire, based on comparative studies of material remains. The French nobleman Anne Claude Philippe, Comte de Caylus, investigated historical changes and cultural connections across the ancient world in his *Collection of Antiquities*, published in seven volumes between 1752 and 1767. The papal prefect of antiquities Johann Joachim Winckelmann outlined the development of ancient art, culminating with the greatness of Greek art, in his *History of the Art of Antiquity*, published in 1764. These and other similar works delivered a model for the transformation of the antiquarian collections into art museums, discussed in Section 1.[38] The comparative approach, especially when applied to countries beyond the Mediterranean, also prompted scholars to reconsider antiquarian assumptions.

2.6 Things outside History

Biblical and mythical history could be written without Moses' handwritings or the Trojan horse. The new histories, on the contrary, depended upon material remains. This made some pasts more accessible than others. Nothing like the Vatican Belvedere existed for the New World. In Spain, large collections were established in the late eighteenth century. In the Americas, they emerged in the nineteenth century, after independence. Before then, collections only contained a limited number of pre-Hispanic artefacts. These were usually catalogued together with other exotic objects from distant parts of the world, as curiosities rather than as antiquities, and with little knowledge of their provenance or original meaning and purpose. Most collectors did not consider them worth preserving. Valuable materials, such as gold or tortoise shell, were reused. Other objects were sold, discarded, or given away.[39]

---

[37] Casaubon, *Treatise*, pp. 97–8. Also, on antiquarianism and history, Miller, *History*, pp. 55–75; Woolf, *Idea of History*, pp. 200–42.
[38] On different uses of antiquities, Sweet, *Antiquaries*; Griggs, 'Universal History'. Also, Harloe, *Winckelmann*; Haskell, *History*.
[39] Feest, 'Collecting'. Also, on Spanish and American collections, Cabello Carro, *Coleccionismo americano*; Earle, 'Monumentos'.

Those interested in the material history of the Americas instead turned to written sources. Only a few accounts, which described pre-Hispanic antiquities in any detail, were available to, or consulted by, the larger scholarly community. European scholars primarily referred to two works: the Jesuit José de Acosta's *Natural and Moral History of the Indies*, and the mestizo Garcilaso de la Vega's *Royal Commentaries of the Incas*, first published in 1590 and 1609. These accounts reflected an emerging antiquarian interest in Spanish America, where scholars investigated Amerindian material remains and thereby questioned the narrow focus of traditional biblical and mythical history on Europe and the Middle East. According to Garcilaso, who was of Incan descent, the Incan Empire played a role in the New World parallel to that of Roman Empire in the Old World, preparing the way for the arrival of Christianity. The Incas, he claimed, had conquered the 'barbarians' of the Andes, who lived in small, isolated communities, some in caves and hollow trees. Their rulers, starting with Manco Capac, transformed these 'barbarians' into human beings, capable of reasoning. They founded cities and introduced agriculture, laws, and a new religion, closer to Christian monotheism. They built magnificent palaces and temples, adorned with gold and silver. Their capital Cuzco, in many ways, compared to Rome and the city's fortress even surpassed, Garcilaso insisted, those seven buildings and statues described as 'wonders of the world'.[40]

Acosta and Garcilaso, nonetheless, viewed Amerindian monuments and artefacts from the perspective of the present. They were not things of the past but associated with the customs and beliefs of contemporary Amerindians. This contemporary world was not a distant wonderland but, like those worlds that Europeans now encountered in Asia and Africa, threatening and haunted by the Devil. The antiquities were idols of the Devil and, as such, did not belong to a particular time or place, but testified to a cosmological battle between good and evil. According to Acosta, Amerindian idolatry had developed over time, from worship of the dead to imagined Gods. However, he based this history on the Book of Wisdom, which had been an inspiration for discussions about idolatry since antiquity. The Devil used similar tricks, and appealed to the same human weaknesses, everywhere. Even in Garcilaso's account, most of the Americas belonged outside of history. The Incas emerged, out of nothing, in a world of fear and idolatry, where people had 'no master but the Devil'. The surrounding people, he claimed, remained in 'that ancient rusticity'. The Incas' more rational religion still opened the door for the Devil and his betrayals. Their

---

[40] Garcilaso, *Commentarios reales*, p. 194; Acosta, *Historia natural*. Also, on American antiquarianism, Franch, *Arqueólogos*; Langebaek, *herederos*, vol. I; Schnapp, 'Ancient Europe'.

temples, shrines, and religious artefacts were not just reminders of a glorious past, but also dangerous forces of evil, which needed to be destroyed.[41]

2.7 Things without History

Eighteenth-century historical works were less concerned about idolatry, but they, nonetheless, differentiated between European and Amerindian antiquities. European antiquities increasingly were revered as things of the past. Amerindian antiquities remained outside of history. Some used the distinction to defend biblical history. One of the most influential eighteenth-century descriptions of the Americas was the Jesuit Joseph-François Lafitau's monumental *Customs of the American Savages Compared to the Customs of the Earliest Times*, published in 1724. Lafitau's book was informed by his missionary work in New France, in today's Canada, from 1712 to 1717. However, his primary purpose was not to explain or justify this work, but instead to counter sceptical critique. The Amerindians, he argued, were descendants of the Greeks and other surrounding people. From these, they had inherited the original revelation, first given to Adam and later passed on by Noah and his sons. They were not heretics or worshippers of the Devil, but, on the contrary, keepers of ancient wisdom, the theology of the earliest times.[42] They proved that divine revelation was not just an invention of Moses or later Jewish scribes.

Lafitau reached this conclusion by comparing classical antiquity with contemporary Amerindians. The Amerindians remained committed to the customs of the ancients, even if in a perverted form. Some of these customs, ancient and modern, were manifested in material objects. A core example was North American tortoise rattles, which he considered parallel to Greek musical instruments (Figure 5). The original inspiration for the lyre, he claimed, had been a dried-out tortoise. However, while Greek instruments had developed, those of the Amerindians had not. After a long discussion of the religious significance of music and dance in antiquity as well as among the Iroquois and Hurons, he tentatively concluded, 'this tortoise of the savages is the same thing as the lyre of Apollo'.[43]

Lafitau's approach to artefacts distinguished him not only from Acosta and Garcilaso but also from the antiquarian tradition. The things did not offer an immediate connection to the past by themselves, but only as parts of a larger interpretative context. The tortoise rattle alone was just another musical instrument, which, as such, had little appeal. It only became significant when

---

[41] Garcilaso, *Commentarios reales*, pp. 13, 11. Also, MacCormack, *Religion*, pp. 249–80; Cervantes, *Devil*, and, on historical inspiration, J.-Rubiés, 'Theology'. For parallel descriptions of South Asian art, Mitter, *Much Maligned Monsters*, pp. 1–72.
[42] Lozar, *Plume*.   [43] Lafitau, *Mœurs*, vol. I, p. 218.

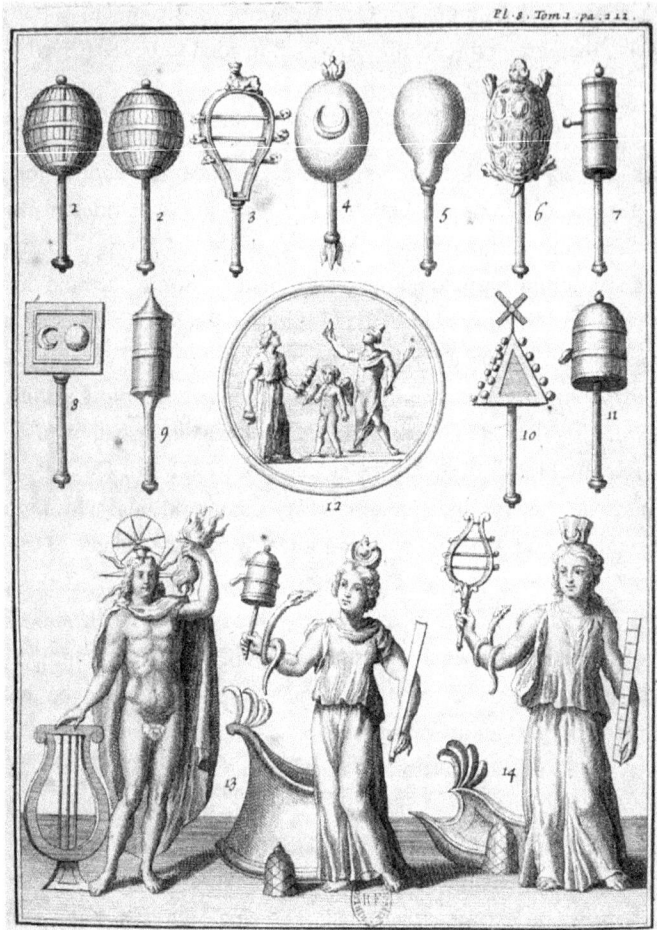

Figure 5 Lafitau's comparison of ancient and Amerindian musical instruments. Number 4, 5, 6, and 10 are Amerindian rattles. The other instruments are from classical antiquity. *Mœurs des sauvages ameriquains compares aux mœurs des premiers temps* (Paris 1724). Courtesy Bibliothèque nationale de France.

compared to other artefacts, texts, and ethnographic observations, which together enabled him to overcome time and reveal a historical world beyond. He illustrated this mediating function on the frontispiece with the writer of history, surrounded by antiquities and books (Figure 6). A putto brings the tortoise rattle and an ancient instrument for comparison. The writer uses them to see beyond father time and reimagine the lost world of Adam and Eve in the Garden of Eden.[44]

---

[44] Also, Certeau, 'Writing'.

Figure 6 Lafitau's frontispiece. *Mœurs des sauvages ameriquains compares aux mœurs des premiers temps* (Paris 1724). Courtesy Bibliothèque nationale de France.

Other eighteenth-century scholars also placed the Amerindians at the beginning of time. Some even questioned whether the great monuments of the Incans and Aztecs had ever existed. The Spaniards, who had reported about these, were no more trustworthy than other historical witnesses. Their testimony also needed material support. The French geographer and mathematician Charles Marie La Condamine stayed in Peru between 1735 and 1743 and visited the ruins of an Incan city. His observations made him question the credibility of Acosta and Garcilaso. Garcilaso, La Condamine reasoned, had written his book in old age, many years after moving to Spain, and probably remembered wrong. The Incas did not know the art of brickmaking. Their buildings were small, only had one floor and no windows. The ruins proved, he argued, turning Garcilaso's account of the rise of the Incas against his vision of a South American Rome, that the inhabitants had been 'savage people' whom the Inca ruler Manco Capac only shorty before had 'pulled out of barbarism' and 'from the depth of the forests'.[45]

2.8 A Global History of Things

For Enlightenment historians who tried to reconstruct world history, without relying on classical myths, the distinction between European and Amerindian artefacts also proved useful. In 1758, the French jurist Antoine-Yves Goguet drafted a new history, reconstructing periods that the sceptical critique had excluded from history, from the Deluge to ancient Greece. For this purpose, he drew upon European antiquarian investigations as well as discussions about material remains around the world. For the situation outside of Europe and the Middle East, he especially relied upon writings about the Americas and constantly referred to Acosta and Garcilaso as well as to Lafitau, La Condamine, and other recent travel writings. He disregarded all speculations about the origins of the Amerindians and instead applied a developmental viewpoint.

Goguet, like Lafitau, was not a traditional antiquary. He was not interested in the things by themselves, or their aesthetic and emotional appeal, but in the historical world that they revealed in comparison. Human development, in his reconstruction, could be divided in stages. Material artefacts documented these stages. One central example was the use of metals. The first metals used by human beings, such as silver and gold, appeared in pure form in nature. They demanded no or little treatment. Only later some people discovered iron, which was harder to mine, purify, and shape. Iron, however, was also the metal that had the greatest impact on human progress. To uncover this history, which was not documented with written sources, he compared 'what could have happened in the first centuries, with the facts that we still have before our eyes', especially in the Americas. The Amerindians had not discovered iron, despite rich deposits of iron ore.[46] This observation also prompted a discussion about stone tools. Bringing together antiquarian works, philological research, and recent travel accounts, Goguet concluded:

> It is known that stone tools were used in America from time immemorial. They have been found in the tombs of the ancient inhabitants of Peru and are still used by many peoples today ... Asia and Europe are scattered with these kinds of stones. They are very often found. There was therefore a time when people of these regions were unaware of the use of iron, like the Americans were before the arrival of the Europeans.[47]

---

[45] Condamine, 'Mémoire', pp. 445–46. Also, Cañizares-Esguerra, *How to Write*, pp. 11–55.
[46] Goguet, *origine*, vol. I, p. 134. Also, Zedelmaier, *Anfang*, pp. 191–213.
[47] Goguet, *origine*, vol. I, p. 148.

Several European historians and philosophers made similar arguments. Pre-Hispanic Amerindians were no longer lost Israelites or wandering Greeks, with a venerable pedigree in biblical and classical history, but outside of time. The Scottish historian William Robertson dismissed speculations about origins. Human beings in similar conditions, he argued, behaved in similar ways. Before Columbus, conditions in the Americas were like those of other primitive people, including the earliest Europeans, and their customs therefore resembled one another. He also questioned whether the Incas and Aztecs were 'civilized' because they 'like the rude tribes around them, were totally unacquainted with the useful metals'.[48] This insistence upon the material basis of world history, however, offered a way back into history.

2.9 Return to History

During the last decades of the eighteenth century, Spanish authorities grew concerned about the place of the Americas in world history. For the Americas to gain a new role, additional sources were needed. In Madrid, the Cosmographer-General of the Indies, Juan Bautista Muñoz, fervently collected manuscripts from Spanish colonies in the Americas and Asia and established an Archive of the Indies. These efforts mirrored the centralization of archives across Europe during the period. However, for Muñoz, the primary motivation was not the consolidation of state power, but historical research. Others in Madrid were looking for artefacts. The soldier and naturalist Antonio de Ulloa, whose description of Incan graves Goguet had relied upon, drafted directions for the collection efforts of the Royal Natural History Cabinet, founded in 1772. Ulloa specifically requested 'antiquities' and remarked that they 'shed light on what the countries were like in the most remote times and through them we gain knowledge of the increase and decrease they have had'. The repeated missions to Palenque reflected these historical concerns. The reports and letters written about the ruins reveal not only the persistence of biblical and mythical history but also the global influence of comparative historical scholarship.[49]

Rumours about the ruins near Palenque first reached Guatemala City in late 1784. A vicar, who was visiting a friend, informed the president of the Royal Audiencia of Guatemala, José Estachería, about the remains of a once prosperous city, rich in spices and gold, in the rainforest. He had not seen the ruins himself but speculated that it could be the biblical city of Ophir. Estachería ordered a local bureaucrat, José Antonio Calderón, to investigate the matter.

---

[48] Robertson, *History*, vol II, p. 268. Also, Meek, *Social Science*.
[49] Ulloa in Cabello Carro, *Coleccionismo americano*, p. 61. Also, on the centralization of archives and historical research, Eskildsen, *Modern Historiography*, pp. 87–105, and, on Muñoz and Palenque, Cañizares-Esguerra, *How to Write*, pp. 193–6, 321–45.

Soon after Calderón reported back that he had indeed found what looked like a great city, with palaces, temples, and streets, possibly once inhabited by the Romans, Carthaginians, or Spaniards, who escaped the Arab invasion of the Iberian Peninsula. Estachería decided for a second expedition, this time headed by the Italian architect Antonio Bernasconi. He also drafted careful and detailed instructions.

Estachería's interests were historical. In his letters about Palenque, he did not mention the dangers of idolatry and seemed unconcerned about the presumed riches of the city. The ruins were potentially things of the past. When he first ordered Calderón to investigate, he described the task as illuminating 'ancient and modern history' and ordered him to investigate 'monuments, epigraphs, inscriptions, statues, and other pieces that indicate more clearly and closely the antiquity, peculiarities, and foundation of that city'.[50] His much more detailed instructions to Bernasconi read like a catalogue over the different ways that antiquities, at the end of the eighteenth century, were used to investigate the past.

The last part of these instructions, concerning architecture, revealed Estachería's inspiration from Enlightenment material histories. He instructed the Italian architect to excavate the foundations of the buildings. This would reveal the inhabitants' level of knowledge of 'civil architecture' and if the city had been built by 'cultured people and not barbarians', which would enable 'appropriate judgements to the illumination of history'. Bernasconi's investigations, Estachería explained, should contribute to a history of architecture, explaining 'the rules which have been successively established in their order by the various nations, and according to the course of the centuries'. After four months, Bernasconi delivered a short and disappointing report. He had little to say about the site and rejected most of Estachería's suggestions. The architecture did not resemble anything he knew, neither ancient nor modern, apart from some arches that looked Gothic. His only general conclusion in this regard was that 'the construction of buildings does not make those who made them completely uncultured in the art'.[51]

The mission did offer some results. Bernasconi sketched a map of the area, architectural plans of a couple buildings, and more accurate drawings of reliefs and decorative details. His report, together with other papers relating to the case, was shipped to Madrid. Muñoz read the material with excitement. He here had proof that La Condamine and others were wrong when they dismissed the testimony of early Spanish historians about buildings in the New World. He also considered it evidence of the existence of an ancient people, superior to those whom the Spanish encountered when they first arrived. Muñoz had some additional questions, mostly about the construction of the buildings,

---

[50] Cabello Carro, *Política*, p. 78.   [51] Ibid., pp. 95–6, 114.

supplementing Estachería's instructions. These questions were shipped back to Guatemala City and Estachería sent the young army captain Antonio del Río to investigate the site again.

2.10 A Global History of Art

The identification of the ruins of Palenque as things of the past soon won broader recognition. Del Río's expedition was followed by others, documenting not only the city in the rainforest but also other ruins and monuments across Mesoamerica. Similar reports emerged from other parts of the world, far from lands known from biblical history. These reports often revered in the rediscovery of unknown artistic and historical worlds among the ruins. The British colonial administrator Thomas Raffles in 1817 described the ancient temples of Java as 'majestic works of art' and noted that they offered proofs of a lost civilization, 'which cannot be falsified'. The colonial officer James Alexander in 1830 similarly praised the caves of Ajanta, in India, as 'magnificent remains of antiquity and wonders of art' and claimed that their fresco paintings documented 'dresses, habits of life, pursuits, general appearance, and even features of the natives of India, perhaps, two thousand or two thousand and five hundred years ago'. In 1845, the artist James Stephanoff imagined a progression of ancient art, based on British Museum's collections and culminating with works from the Parthenon, but also including some artefacts that he only knew from travel accounts (Figure 7). At the bottom, in an imaginary and achronological 'Earliest Period', were Mayan reliefs from Palenque and Copan to the sides and statues from Java and India in the middle.[52]

The travel accounts also influenced historical scholarship. In 1842, the Berlin professor Franz Kugler published *Handbook of Art History*, which described art from across the world and included a chapter on 'The old monuments of America'. Kugler did not place the Americas in some imaginary beginning, like Stephanoff and others before him. When the Europeans arrived, he explained, the Amerindians had been through a long historical process, with ancient greatness and later decay, and 'great monuments of art stood there as witnesses of these particular cultural circumstances'. The Spanish had destroyed much, but enough remained to reconstruct 'an independent development of the people' and to prove 'the originality of their art'. The art of Palenque, with which he concluded the chapter, exemplified both independence and historical changes, as an art form already beyond its perfection and in decline.[53]

---

[52] Raffles, *History*, vol. II, p. 6. Alexander, 'Notice', p. 365. Also, on Mesoamerica, Evans, *Romancing* and, on India, Mitter, *Much Maligned Monsters*, pp. 105–88. On Stephanoff, Jenkins, *Archaeologists*, pp. 61–63.

[53] Kugler, *Handbuch*, pp. 18, 22, 23.

Figure 7 James Stephanoff's imaginary history of art (74 x 62 cm), from bottom to top. 'An Assemblage of Works of Art, from the Earliest Period to the Time of Phydias'. Watercolour, 1845. Courtesy The Trustees of the British Museum, United Kingdom.

Some people were still left out. Africa south of Sahara was not mentioned at all. For South America, Kugler only discussed the Incas. The antiquities of North America, above Mexico, he briefly dismissed as reflecting 'the simplest cultural condition'. Maybe more unsettling for his readers, he declared this condition as parallel to 'that of Northern European antiquity'. The ancient Incas and Mesoamericans entered world history, but the ancient Germans remained outside, as primitives with simple stone tools and burial mounds, and not much more. Kugler discussed these remains, but as examples of the early beginnings of art, which were similar all over the world.[54] His views of art and history were still shaped by an antiquarian tradition, privileging the aesthetics of Greco-Roman antiquity. For Northern European antiquity, as well as most of Africa and the Americas, to return to world history, a different approach was needed. The next section explores how scholars arrived at an approach, which demanded that artefacts from all over the world were gathered in museums in Europe and North America. This provoked new debates about who could contribute to the world history of things and, therefore, had a claim to the material remains.

3 Assembling the World

3.1 The Muisca Gold Raft

During the early 1880s, Liborio Zerda, a medical doctor who taught natural sciences at the University of the Rosary in Bogotá, Colombia, visited several private collections, pursuing remains of the pre-Hispanic past. He was especially infatuated with one artefact, a small gold figure, belonging to the wife of the banker Salomón Koppel (Figure 8). The figure was the only known depiction of the ceremony consecrating a ruler of the Muisca, the indigenous population of the Cundiboyacense high plateau in the Andes mountains. It showed him on a raft, surrounded by attendants and oarsmen, bringing gold offerings to the Gods, on Lake Guatavita. This ceremony was the origin of the legend of the golden realm, El Dorado, which awakened Spanish greed and unleashed the destruction of Muisca society. The figure also, to Zerda, was a key to this lost world, revealing their technical ingenuity, social order, and religious worldviews.[55]

Zerda wanted not only to know this past but also to convince his compatriots that, despite centuries of iconoclasm and plunder, such knowledge was still possible. The pre-Hispanic people of Colombia had not left written sources or great buildings, like those of the Mesoamericans and the Incas, and many other ancient people around the world, but some of their arts and crafts remained. The golden realm had not yet entirely disappeared. His ongoing investigations were published in a series, entitled 'El Dorado', in a new literary journal, published by the artist and intellectual Alberto Urdaneta. The series was richly illustrated with engravings of objects, such as the gold raft, discussed in the articles.[56]

---

[54] Ibid., p. 19. Also, for a different reading, Bredekamp, 'Franz Kugler'.
[55] Zerda, *El Dorado*, 1972, vol. I, pp. 32–5. Also, Botero, *redescubrimiento*, pp. 85–87, Langebaek, *herederos,* vol. I., pp. 296–303.
[56] Also, on the journal, Moreno de Ángel, 'Papel Periódico Ilustrado'.

Figure 8 The Muisca gold raft (9 x 17 cm in diameter) in the private collection of Salomón Koppel and his wife. Unknown artist. Photo by Julio Racines Bernal. Courtesy Museo Nacional de Colombia.

During the nineteenth century, the yearning for things of the past was spreading across the entire world, embracing more and more diverse artefacts. Objects, which previously had been ignored, only exploited for their material value, or destroyed as idols of the Devil, gained new significance. In Colombia, Zerda was not the first to suggest that they revealed the country's distant past. In 1856, while curators in Europe were still pondering whether such artefacts deserved attention, the young poet José Joaquín Borda published an essay in Bogotá, which discussed the recent European 'fanaticism' of museums and proposed a new Colombian historical museum. 'Where', Borda complained, 'are the immense treasures of our immense and rich territory? Where are the memories of those venerable indigenous races that before the conquest covered the land inhabited by us today?' By the 1880s, these concerns had acquired new urgency. Pre-Hispanic artefacts were rapidly being bought up not only by local antiquaries, but also by Europeans and North Americans. Zerda's initiative was a reaction to a recent visit by the director of the Ethnographic Museum in Berlin, Adolf Bastian. During his six months stay in Colombia, Bastian fervently collected artefacts and shipped many boxes back. He also tried to acquire the gold raft. A few years later, he convinced Koppel to sell. On its way to Berlin, the raft was lost in a warehouse fire in the German port city of Bremen.[57]

3.2 History of Prehistory

The Göttingen professor August Ludwig Schlözer coined the word 'prehistory' in 1772. Schlözer was an Enlightenment thinker with a cosmopolitan outlook, but also an empiricist. History should be based upon reliable evidence and, as suggested in the French Royal Academy of Inscriptions and Belles-Lettres earlier in the century, periods without written sources did not belong. 'I am allowed', he insisted, 'to separate the entire history, from the beginning of the world to the beginning of Rome, or rather the poor leftovers of it, from the rest of world history, and to call it prehistory'. Other parts of the world entered history later than Rome. The Americas only entered with the arrival of Europeans in the fifteenth century, Northern Europe, above the Elbe and beyond the Donau, with Christianity in the ninth century. Before the ninth century, there was: 'No internal history, since the art of writing was still not in the North' and 'No external history, since the North still had no connection of the South'.[58] Such statements became more common as the historical discipline focused its efforts on archival research. By the early nineteenth century, the biblical and mythical world histories had lost all academic credibility, and, to many historians, documents became the only way to revive the past. Without surviving written sources, the past was forever lost. As the Berlin professor Leopold von Ranke explained his students in 1831:

> In and for itself, history embraces the life of humankind through all times. However, all too much of this is lost or unknown ... Some of what has been

---

[57] Borda, 'Museo', pp. 46–7. Also, on the raft, Botero, *redescubrimiento*, pp. 148–50, and, for global context, Marchand, 'Dialectics'.
[58] Schlözer, *Vorstellung*, vol. I, p. 67, *Einleitung*, p. 5.

described is lost, some has never been described – all this is draped with death; only those, whom history considers, are not entirely dead, their essence and existence still act, when they are understood: with the loss of memory the actual death emerges. Fortunate, where documentary traces still remain. At least these can be considered. But when not? For example, in the earliest history? I think that this should be excluded from history, for good reasons, as it contradicts its principle, which is documentary research.[59]

Other scholars, especially in Northern Europe, insisted that these periods should not be discarded. Through material remains, 'prehistory' remained accessible. Some also appropriated the language of archives and documents to explain the significance of these remains. In 1806, the Copenhagen professor Rasmus Nyerup proposed the establishment of a Danish National Museum. The distant past, he admitted, was hidden 'in a thick fog'. However, antiquities, stored in the alternative 'archive' of the earth, could be read as 'documents'. It was still possible 'to study our forefathers' tools and crafts and, at least, spell through some chapters' of the history of antiquity. The next year, Nyerup became secretary of the new Danish Royal Commission for the Preservation of Antiquities. In 1811, he also acquired the prehistoric collections from the Royal Cabinet of Curiosities and established a study collection in the university library.[60]

In 1816, the Copenhagen businessman Christian Jürgensen Thomsen replaced Nyerup as secretary of the commission. Thomsen transformed the study collection into the Royal Museum of Nordic Antiquities, which opened in 1819. He organized the artefacts into typological categories and developmental series. Most famously, he divided them between Stone Age, Bronze Age, and Iron Age (Figure 9). This division reminded of earlier philosophical histories, especially Antoine-Yves Goguet's conjectures about stone and metal tools, discussed in Section 2. However, to Thomsen, the artefacts were not just filling a hole between the Deluge and ancient Greece or saving periods without written sources. They allowed him to access the past in a new way and were 'collected and compared, capable of giving us a more graphic presentation of the forefathers' religion, culture, external life, and more, than written sources'. This history was not limited to the three ages but covered many smaller developmental stages within. Stone tools were not just stone tools but became gradually more refined and polished before they were replaced by bronze. Ornamentation slowly evolved over time. These changes revealed cultural differences, patterns of migration, and networks of trade. So, prehistory had a history.[61]

---

[59] Ranke, *Aus Werk und Nachlass*, vol. IV, p. 84. Also, Eskildsen, *Modern Historiography*, pp. 87–105.
[60] Nyerup, *Historisk-statistiske Skildring*, pp. 1, 3.
[61] Thomsen, 'Kortfattet Udsigt', p. 27. Also, Eskildsen, 'Language'.

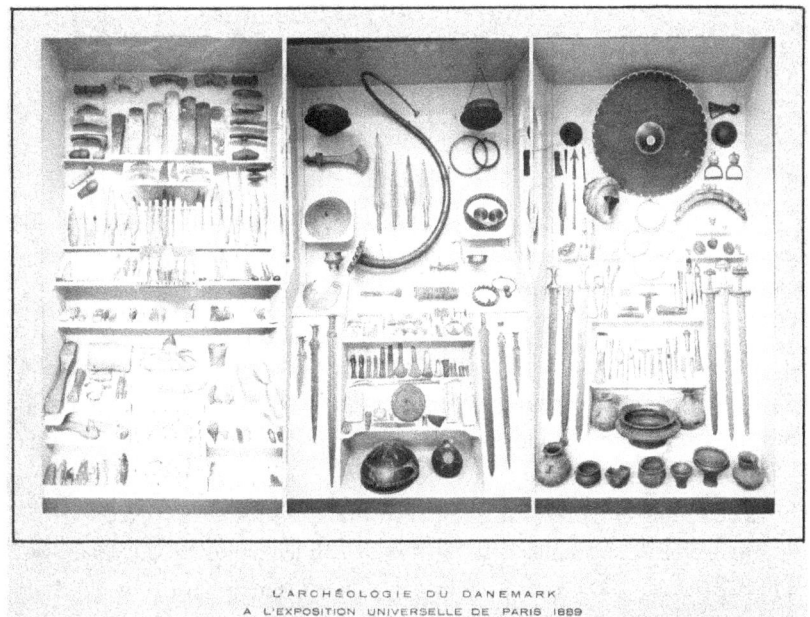

Figure 9 The Royal Museum of Nordic Antiquities' exhibits of Stone Age, Bronze Age, and Iron Age at the World Exhibition in Paris in 1889. Courtesy Danmarks Oldtid, Nationalmuseet, Denmark.

Thomsen's work provoked heated debates across Europe. Some questioned if history could be written solely based on material objects. Many defend more eclectic and open definitions of archaeology, insisting upon closer connections to historical research on written sources. Others found inspiration in racial theories and comparative anatomy, and investigated human remains. Among scholars working with artefacts, however, Thomsen's Three-Age-System was gradually accepted and applied in different European countries. A prominent advocate was the British polymath John Lubbock, whose *Pre-historic Times* offered a popular introduction to comparative archaeology. After its first publication in 1865, the book was repeatedly republished and translated into several languages. Lubbock refined the Three-Age-System, subdividing the Stone Age between an early Paleolithic Period and a later Neolithic Period. An early follower of Charles Darwin, he also connected technological and cultural development to biological evolution and employed the system for global comparisons.[62]

---

[62] Lubbock, *Pre-historic Times*. For an overview, Trigger, *History*, on Lubbock, pp. 147–8, 171–76. Also, on the dissemination of the Three-Age-System, Rowley-Conwy, *Genesis*.

3.3 World History in Museums

As early as the 1830s, Thomsen speculated if his curatorial approach could be applied outside of Europe and, for comparison, exhibited artefacts from the South Pacific and North America next to Nordic prehistoric ones. He assumed control of the ethnographic collections of the Royal Cabinet of Curiosities in 1839 and collected many additional objects from around the world. By 1849, the collection had swollen so much that he opened a Royal Ethnographic Museum, occupying forty-four rooms in a former castle. In the ethnographic exhibits, like in those for Nordic prehistory, he ordered people according to stages, distinguishing between those without metals, with metals but without writing, and with both metals and writing. The placement depended upon their situation when they first came into close contact with Europeans. Greenland was in the first category, without metals, and Africa south of Sahara in the second category, with metals but without writing. The exhibits also showed later changes, resulting from the encounter with Europeans and technological advancements. No part of the world was outside of history. The collections, he claimed in 1844, 'show the gradual development of culture, give useful inklings to the history researcher and the geographer, and also make us aware of the affect that descent, climate, culture, religion, estate, and other circumstances have upon man'.[63]

From the mid nineteenth century, several countries founded ethnographic and colonial museums. The primary purpose of these museums was to document and display the human and natural resources available in European possessions abroad. Several curators, however, shared Thomsen's historical ambitions. His most important successor was the Berlin professor Adolf Bastian, who in 1876 became director of the New Museum's prehistoric and ethnographic collections and later of the Royal Ethnographic Museum, officially founded in 1873, but first opened in 1886. Bastian worked with great determination to document world history by enlarging the collections. During his years as director, the museum became the largest such institution, surpassing not only the museum in Copenhagen but also those of larger colonial powers. In 1898, a curator at the British Museum estimated that the collections in Berlin were 'six or seven times as extensive' as those in London. Many of Bastian's acquisitions came from German colonies. Others were bought on the market, donated, or collected by Bastian and his assistants on numerous journeys around the world.[64]

One goal of Bastian's collection efforts was to 'salvage' material, from living traditions around the world. The arrival of Europeans opened a short window of

---

[63] Thomsen, *Kort Udsigt*, p. 37. Also, on the exhibits, Steinhauer, *Kort Veiledning*.
[64] Penny, *Objects*, quote from the British museum, p. 1. Also, Penny, *Humboldt's Shadow*; Hoffmann, *Museum*. For context, Kuper, *Museum*.

opportunity before people changed their ways. So, the task was, in Bastian's words, to 'collect everything' while still possible. Parallel efforts happened within Europe, where Bastian's close collaborator Rudolf Virchow gathered traditional German crafts, which 'modern culture' now threatened with 'annihilation'. Also here, Virchow explained, it was necessary 'to act quickly, and to salvage what still can be salvaged at all'.[65] Another goal was to uncover remains of early human developments. In this regard, Bastian was especially preoccupied with the Americas. Already before Columbus, 'historical people', who advanced culturally and socially, emerged in South and Central America. However, because of the absence of written sources, he argued, 'the collection must in this case, as with natural tribes without writing, step in as the *conditio sine qua non* if the study is to be started at all'. So, a huge collection of pre-Hispanic artefacts was a necessary foundation for his new world history. By 1880, before German colonial expansion, which shifted attention towards Africa and the South Pacific, Amerindian artefacts constituted more than half of the collections. Bastian's first large collecting mission for the museum, from May 1875 to August 1876, went to the Americas. The museum already owned over five thousand Mexican artefacts, but only a few hundred from South America. He concentrated his efforts here. During the journey, he spent six months in Colombia alone.[66]

3.4 Prehistory in Collections

The congress of New Grenada, later Colombia, in 1833 permitted the free exploration of pre-Hispanic remains. Everyone could excavate and sell their findings to whomever they wanted. The remains were no longer idols of the Devil, which needed to be destroyed, but simply material resources to be exploited. The law started a gold rush, elevating looters of sacred sites, *guaqueros*, into a profession. The many antiquities on the market also invigorated local antiquarianism. Several prominent collectors were in the Antioquia region, at the centre of the gold rush. Some, like the chemist Vicente Restrepo, whose laboratory in Medellín checked the quality of gold findings, were themselves involved. The largest collection belonged to the Medellín businessman Leocadio María Arango. In his private museum, Arango exhibited not only pre-Hispanic gold work, ceramics, and stone tools, but also fossils, metals, minerals, gemstones, rare insects, moths and butterflies, bird-nests and eggs, and hundreds of stuffed birds. Like many antiquaries, he revelled in the beauty of the objects. The

---

[65] Bastian, *Heilige Sage*, pp. vii–viii, Virchow, 'Verwaltungsbericht', p. 729, On Virchow's collections, Müller, 'Sammlungskonzeption'.
[66] Bastian 'Bedeutung', pp. 104, 99. On Bastian's journey, Fischer, 'Adolf Bastian's Travels'; Botero, *redescubrimiento,* pp. 140–68.

gold figures were exhibited on black velvet cloth. The many birds were mounted in colourful dioramas, behind glass in display cases of noble woods.[67]

When Bastian arrived in Colombia in October 1875, he entered this network of *guaqueros* and private collectors. Whenever he came to a new place, he inquired about antiquities and these questions inevitably led him to local antiquaries. Most did not mind his extractive approach and gladly sold and even donated artefacts to the German scientist. Others were equally willing to sell. In the small town of Neira, Bastian reported how, while having breakfast with the local doctor, rumours spread about his interests and, when returning to his lodgings in the afternoon, 'people approached me from different houses with antiquities that they had gathered in the meantime'. Bastian also visited recently opened pre-Hispanic graves and described the professional language of the *guaqueros*. His travel journal, however, says little about his conversations with native Colombians. During his visit to Medellín, he briefly mentioned Arango but only noted that he had seen his museum and made 'some interesting acquisitions'.[68]

While in Bogotá, Bastian stayed at the house of the German ambassador. On 15 February 1876, he here delivered a lecture, outlining the purpose of his travels. Since independence, Bastian declared, scientists had explored the natural abundance of Colombia. He instead hunted for a heretofore undiscovered treasure: 'the *authentic documents of its ancient history*'. These 'documents', he further explained, were not written on paper, but consisted of 'antiquities, still preserved under the earth'. Scholars had now figured out how to read them and uncover a new 'universal history', which covered not only Europe and the Middle East, but all of humankind. For this universal history to emerge, however, the antiquities must be 'incorporated in scientific institutes, in the museums of Europe and America, to explain each other by way of comparison'.[69] So, Colombia had a pre-Hispanic history, but the full comprehension of this history demanded that the artefacts entered large scientific museums, with collections from many parts of the world. These only existed outside of the country.

3.5 Prehistory in the Paper Museum

In Bogotá, Bastian's lecture provoked discussions and proposals for new approaches to pre-Hispanic artefacts, including Zerda's 'El Dorado' series, launched in March 1882. Zerda here challenged Bastian's monopoly on interpreting

---

[67] Arango, *Catálogo*. For descriptions, Brisson, *Viajes*, pp. 72–73; Espagnat, *Souvenirs*, pp. 281–84; Fuhrmann and Mayor, *Voyage*, pp. 43–44; Hoyes, 'Museo'. Also, Botero, *redescubrimiento*, pp. 75–79, and, on antiquarianism in Antioquia, Piazzini, 'Guaqueros', pp. 49–78.
[68] Bastian, *Culturländer*, vol. I, pp. 285, 269.
[69] Excerpt in Zerda, *El Dorado*, 1883, pp. ix–x. Emphasis in the original. Also, Bastian, *Culturländer*, vol. I, p. 333.

the pre-Hispanic past. He initially explained some basic ideas of comparative archaeology, including Thomsen's Three-Age System, and their local relevance. Zerda knew these theories through the writings of John Lubbock, but he emphasized technological and cultural development over biological evolution. Before the Spanish arrived, he argued, the territories of Colombia had already been through a long development. Like in Europe, it was possible to subdivide the Stone Age into different, gradually more refined, stages. The country had also entered the Bronze Age and used different metals not only for tools and weapons but also to perpetuate 'the memory of their customs, their myths and religious ceremonies, whose origin was long before the Bronze Age'. Amerindians, especially the Muisca, had established advanced societies and were in close contact with Incas to the south and the Mesoamericans to the north. They had not progressed to the Iron Age, but, nonetheless, had a diverse and rich history.[70]

This history, he demonstrated, was accessible through private collections in Colombia. He often mentioned local antiquaries and allowed his readers to enter their collections virtually. One engraving reproduced ceramics from Cundinamarca and Antioquia exactly as they were exhibited in the private collection of Danish consul in Bogotá, Bendix Koppel (Figure 10). Different artefacts were casually placed on a table, some leaning on others, and a couple on an elevated platform in the middle. This setting was circumstantial and unnecessary for transforming the ceramics into things of the past. A few years later, the German archaeologist Max Uhle reproduced several of the same artefacts. Uhle presented them isolated and on a uniform background, as scientific specimens, representing types.[71] Zerda instead emphasised the local antiquarian context and, through the engraving, transformed the intimate experience of the private collection into a public viewing.

In this public viewing, the objects changed meaning. Zerda explained their original purpose and place in his larger history of Colombia. Engravings of other objects were used for comparative investigations. In 1882, a Muisca sacred site, or *huaca*, was discovered in Chirajara, near the town of Quetame, and Urdaneta acquired several objects. These were again reproduced as exhibited in the collection, but Zerda noted similarities to other objects. One of the figures recalled the attendants on Salomón Koppel's gold raft. Together they revealed some of the symbols of authority in Muisca society. Zerda exclaimed, 'without any exaggeration we can say that the *Chirajara huaca* is a history book whose cover is made of clay and whose characters are made of gold. Let us therefore open this book and

---

[70] Zerda, *El Dorado*, 1972, vol. I, p. 13. On Zerda's interpretation of Lubbock, also Langebaek, *herederos,* vol. I., pp. 296–304.
[71] Ibid., pp. 173–9, Uhle, *Kultur*, vol. I. Julio Racines Bernal photographed the same exhibition in Koppel's private collection. For this photo, MS No. 4929, MN.

Figure 10 Engraving of ceramics from Cundinamarca and Antioquia in Bendix Koppel's private collection. *El Papel Periódico Ilustrado* (5 July 1883). Courtesy Banco de la República, Colombia.

study in it'.[72] So, his paper museum was reviving the past and proving that a historical museum was possible. The artefacts did not need to leave for Europe and North America to write the pre-Hispanic history of Colombia.

Other voices joined in as well. The Cuban-born journalist Rafael María Merchan wrote several essays on pre-Hispanic antiquities in Bogotá journals and newspapers. One of these essays, published in 1886, advocated new public attention to the issue. Zerda and the novelist Jorge Isaacs, who had been investigating the indigenous tribes of Magdalena state 'with the passion of the antiquary', proved that Colombia had 'competent men' who could lead such an effort. However, the government had 'shamefully abandoned' the study and preservation of antiquities. The National Museum was underfunded and 'deficient'. Private collections, such as that of Gonzalo Ramos Ruiz which was sold in 1882 and eventually ended up in Bastian's Ethnographic Museum in Berlin, were allowed to leave the country. This would 'one day be a cause of national remorse'.[73]

While Bogotá intellectuals imagined a historical museum on paper, the first steps were taken in Medellín. As early as the 1870s, Arango may have been dreaming about a historical museum. In 1877, he sent a gold tumbaga figure to Berlin and asked Bastian for Assyrian, Persian, or Egyptian objects in return. Around the same time, he started collecting a kind of ceramics, unlike other known pre-Hispanic

---

[72] Zerda, *El Dorado*, 1972, vol. I, p. 68.   [73] Merchan, 'Antiguedades Americanas', p. 3.

artefacts, emerging on the market in Medellín. Arango was convinced that these represented 'a civilization that had already disappeared when the conquest took place'. So, even without artefacts from the Old World, he could document changes over time. One French visitor, passing through Medellin in 1897–8, noted that one in his private museum could find the 'entire history of Indian land', which was 'written in terracotta and gold, summarized much more completely than in Bogotá, along three or four rooms'. This history started with 'its dark origin marked by vases with the crude heads of dogs or monkeys' and ended with the Spanish conquest.[74] Apart from dogs and monkeys, and many frogs, the ceramics also included aquatic and imaginary creatures, which Arango associated with the mythology of the ancient civilization (Figure 11).

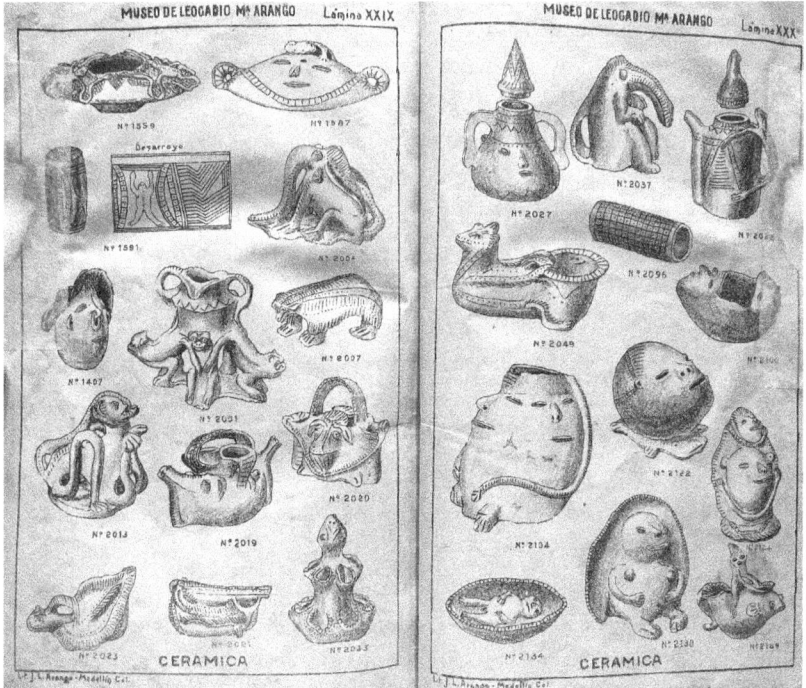

Figure 11 Ceramic figures in Leocadio María Arango's private museum in Medellin. *Catalogo del Museo del Sr. Leocadio María Arango* (Medellín: Imprenta Oficial, 1905), Lámina XXIV-XXX. Courtesy Biblioteca Luis Ángel Arango, Colombia.

---

[74] Arango, *Catálogo*, p. 10; Espagnat, *Souvenirs,* p. 281. Also, on Bastion, Botero, *redescubrimiento*, p. 147.

3.6 Prehistory in the Museum

During the first decades of the nineteenth century, many recently independent South and Central American countries founded museums. The Colombian government in 1823 established a Natural History Museum. Several artefacts considered important for history of the new state, such as battle trophies and memorabilia of Simón Bolivar, soon entered the museum and it was renamed National Museum. The museum was later divided into three sections: natural history; history, archaeology, and curiosities; and paintings. In 1881, the scientist Fidel Pombo produced the first museum catalogue, reflecting these priorities. The complaints of Bogotá intellectuals, however, were justified. In Pombo's catalogue, history only concerned the period after Spanish conquest and especially after independence. Prehistoric and ethnographic artefacts filled less than one page, under the heading 'indigenous objects and curiosities', and were only briefly mentioned as types or in topological categories, such as 'Very curious comb' and 'Idols and clay vessels', without any further discussion of their age, meaning, or provenance. The only exception was an Amerindian cloak, assumed to have belonged to the wife of the last Incan emperor.[75]

During the early 1880s, the interest in the pre-Hispanic past put pressure on the National Museum. As early as May 1881, the Colombian congress passed a new law regarding the museum. Among its tasks was now to collect and preserve objects 'that serve as documents to clarify the primitive history of the country'. In September the same year, the Secretary of Public Instruction, Ricardo Becerra, wrote to local governments around the country and requested donations, as an aid to the reorganization. The first item on his wish list was artefacts 'that represent the races of our country and its state of civilization prior to the conquest, and in particular those that serve to clarify the still obscure problems of Colombian ethnology'. At the end of October, the museum reported receiving several donations.[76]

In 1886, Pombo published a larger expanded catalogue. The prehistorical and ethnographic artefacts were still a side note to the much larger historical collections, but he now treated these with equal seriousness and discussed their historical value. The artefacts were not just curiosities, but things of the past, potentially revealing a world that otherwise would be inaccessible. The country had been inhabited long before the arrival of Europeans, but, Pombo explained, the Spanish had 'annihilated' these people 'without trying to get to know them and leave us more information about their social life, their industry,

---

[75] Pombo, *Breve Guia*, pp. 12, 13. Also, Rodríguez Prada, *Musée National*, pp. 378–89; 'Museos'. For context, Earle, 'Monumentos'.

[76] 'Ley 34', p. 48, Becerra, 'Circular'; Caicedo Rojas, *Informe*.

and their productions'. They had therefore been inaccessible for historians, working only from written sources. There was no other way to 'complete our ancient history' and obtain 'explanation of the unknown' than by investigating the material remains. Therefore 'all of those ancient objects which belonged to the aborigines of Colombia' should be 'permanently deposited in the National Museum'. The changes in Pombo's catalogue reflected a larger transformation of Colombian historical understanding. Many scholars embraced evolutionary theories, and propagated racist viewpoints, but historical works also increasingly considered the pre-Hispanic past as integral to Colombian history. The interpretation of this pre-Hispanic past would become a central and divisive issue in Colombian politics throughout the twentieth century.[77]

3.7 Faking and Trading Histories

During the first decades of the twentieth century, a scandal slowly gathered steam among archaeologists and ethnologists. A large amount of unusual pottery from the Cauca Valley, around Medellín, arrived in museums and collections across the world. Some questioned their authenticity. The American Museum of Natural History in New York, which had acquired a considerable collection, asked different experts for their opinions and decided that they were genuine on the words of 'reputable travelers' and collectors, and because of 'a small lot of the same pottery with a certification of its antiquity by Leocadio M. Arango'. In May 1920, however, the Medellín scholar Juan Bautista Montoya y Flórez, who previously had authenticated Arango's collection, ended the discussion. He revealed in a Bogotá newspaper that a family in Medellín had produced the pottery.[78] They were also behind the pieces that made Arango speculate about an ancient civilization, which had disappeared before Spanish conquest.

The father of the family, Julián Alzate, was a hunter and taxidermist, who provided specimens of natural history to Arango and other collectors in Medellín. He discovered that pre-Hispanic artefacts were a better business and, together with his sons, started large-scale production. They baked the ceramics in a darker colour, instead of fresh red pottery, and then covered them with diluted yellow earth, to appear as if they had been underground. Sometimes they put stones inside, suggesting hidden treasures. The family members had different styles. The aquatic and imaginary figures, which inspired Arango to think about ancient mythology, may have been the invention of one of the sons, Miguel, who preferred such motifs.[79]

---

[77] Pombo, *Nueva Guia*, p. 119. On curatorial practices, which only changed later, Botero, *redescubrimiento*, pp. 198–201; Reyes Gavilán, 'Entre curiosidades'. On race and history writing in twentieth-century Colombia, Langebaek, *herederos*, vol. II.
[78] Mead, 'South America', p. 333. Also, López Lugo, 'Autentificar'.
[79] Vélez Vélez, 'Apuntes anecdoticos'.

The international success of the Alzate family evidenced the emergence of a market for world art. In both Paris and New York, a private market appeared during the second half of the nineteenth century. The artefacts were sold as antiquities, not just curiosities, and shops provided an atmosphere of old age, with medieval or colonial wooden façades, archaic names, and dim lighting. Global networks of dealers catered to the demand. This market also encouraged the production of fakes. Counterfeits on the antiquities market were nothing new. Forgery had been a faithful companion to European antiquarianism from the beginning. An early case involved Michelangelo, who in his youth once disguised a new statue, to make it appear as excavated from a ground, and then sold it in Rome as an antiquity. During the following centuries, European antiquaries and scholars frequently complained about the forgery industry. Now, forgeries appeared from all over world.[80]

Some were made in Europe and shipped to Pacific Islands, to be 'discovered' and sold back. Others were produced in the countries of origin. After her visit to Egypt in 1873, the English novelist Amelia Edwards reported about the large forgery industry and claimed that local dealers sold 'more forgeries than genuine antiquities'. In 1884, a French handbook for collectors similarly warned about the many forgeries arriving from Mexico. In Paris, the book noted, one honest antiquity dealer even had a category in his catalogue with 'Counterfeit Mexican idols, 5 to 25 francs'. The Alzate family also found customers on this market. New York, one museum director claimed, was 'flooded' with their ceramics 'which were sold in several places in the city, notably in one of the largest department stores, minimum price being twenty-five cents each'.[81]

After the Alzate scandal, Colombia no longer played the same role as provider of antiquities. In many countries, European hoarding inspired laws protecting artefacts that remained in the country. From the seventeenth century, the Papel State in Rome introduced several antiquities laws. After Napoleon's plunder, Pope Pius VII in 1802 prohibited export of ancient artefact. Lord Elgin's defacement of the Parthenon provoked outrage in Greece and, in 1827, while still fighting for independence, the Greek National Assembly passed a law banning exports. The Ottoman Empire introduced such laws in 1872 and 1884, the latter in reaction to recent exploits of German archaeologists. Colombia followed suit in 1918 and passed a law, declaring pre-Hispanic monuments and artefacts 'an integral part of the material of national history'. In 1920, another law prohibiting export, even if the artefacts were privately owned.[82] The free and legal exploitation, which

---

[80] On the market, Charpy, 'Trading Places'; Jacobs, *Plunder?* pp. 74–126. On historical fakes, Eskildsen, 'Fälschung'. On art fakes, Lenain, *Art Forgery*.
[81] Edwards, *Thousand Miles*, p. 601; Eudel, *Truquage*, p. 54; Saville, 'Blackware Pottery', p. 146.
[82] 'Ley 48', p. 98 and 'Ley 47'. Also, for earlier laws, Marchand, 'Dialectics'.

started with the 1833 law allowing everyone to excavate pre-Hispanic sites, finally ended. Vendors of antiquities, however, turned to other sources as well as illegal means of acquisition. The private market for world art, as discussed in the next section, only expanded during the twentieth century. This market found support in a form of historical scholarship, which divided the world between those truly yearning for the things of the past and those who did not. All parts of the world may have a history, but, some argued, not everyone had the same connection to the past or an equal appreciation of its material remains.

4 Dividing the World
4.1 The Nok Terracotta Head

At the beginning the twentieth century, the British military gained control of the Jos Plateau, in the recently established Northern Nigeria Protectorate, and its vast tin deposits, previously mined by indigenous groups. In the decades after, European companies opened hundreds of mines, digging from the surface, removing tons of rust-red earth, before reaching the tin-bearing stratum several meters down. Terracotta figures started showing up. Some miners just destroyed the figures or threw them away. They were looking for tin, not art. In one case, a human head, broken from a larger statue, was used as a scarecrow, to protect a yams field from birds (Figure 12). The head in the spring of 1944 caught the attention of a local colonial administrator, Bernard Fagg, who had studied archaeology at Cambridge. It reminded him of a monkey head, in the collection of the Department of Mines, found near the village of Nok. He decided that the findings were connected, belonging to the 'Nok culture', and probably very old. Today, they are considered the oldest surviving sub-Saharan figurative sculptures, produced for over a thousand years, from around a millennium BC and into the first centuries AD.[83]

In 1951, the Art Gallery of the Imperial Institute in London exhibited three figures, representing the 'Prehistoric culture of Nok', including the former scarecrow, then in Fagg's private collection. The curator was his brother, William Fagg, who worked at the British Museum. In a lecture the same year, he briefly explained the historical significance. African art had often been considered as derivative. The discovery finally disproved such theories. The 'Nok culture', he argued, 'reveals a great range of stylizations of the human form in terra-cotta sculptures of the first quality and many sizes'. In addition,

---
[83] On Nok culture and its discovery, Breunig, *Nok*. Also, on mining, Morrison, 'Early Tin Production'.

Figure 12 Human terracotta head (22 cm x 17 cm), found in a tin mine near Jemaa in 1943 and used as a scarecrow, which prompted Bernard Fagg to propose an early 'Nok culture'. Unknown artist. Courtesy National Commission for Museums and Monuments, Nigeria.[84]

several findings could be 'reasonably dated, on geological grounds, before the birth of Christ'. It was therefore no longer possible to postulate 'a gradual

---

[84] https://doi.org/10.71556/nmlagos99.

degeneration from some high art borrowed from some great civilization'.[85] Africa had its own history and artistic legacies.

The Nok figures were only the latest of a series of historical surprises. Until the end of the nineteenth century, most of Africa, apart from coastal colonies, remained outside European control. Then, over a few decades, in the so-called 'Scramble for Africa', almost the entire continent was conquered. As Europeans moved inland, they also stumbled upon other historical worlds. The lands around the Niger Delta proved abundant. In 1897, British Royal Marines destroyed the ancient capital of the Kingdom of Benin, murdered many of its inhabitants, and looted its treasures, accumulated over centuries. As the loot was sold, ivory carvings and bronze castings, documenting artistic traditions going back to the Middle Ages, flooded European museums and private collections. In 1910, the German explorer Leo Frobenius visited the holy city of Ile-Ife and reported back about stunning naturalistic sculptures, even older than those of Benin. Other findings followed, culminating with the Nok figures. Many of these had always been known to Africans. Most of the artworks stolen from Benin were carefully preserved in the palace of the Oba, or King. Frobenius noted that the Yoruba honoured and revered the people of Ile-Ife as 'owners of the oldest monuments'.[86] However, the antiquities now became familiar to Europeans.

By the mid twentieth century, it was becoming evident that people everywhere had undergone changes over time and had produced artefacts, testifying to these changes. All over the world, including in many colonies, museums and other institutions collected, preserved, and exhibited these material remains. This also resulted in new competition for the things. Many, especially as colonies gained independence, started discussing to whom they rightfully belonged. In April 1966, the Senegalese president Léopold Sédar Senghor organized the First World Festival of Negro Arts, in Dakar, which emphasized the importance of African arts for the future development of the continent. The festival opened with a colloquium on the 'Function and Significance of African Negro Art in the Life of the People and for the People'. William Fagg, still representing the British Museum, was among the speakers. Unlike other participants, he questioned the aims of the festival. Africa had its own history and artistic legacies, but, he argued, Africans did not have any special claims to the remains. The 'People', in whose life the artefacts now had 'Function and Significance', were primarily Europeans. African art, he explained, 'does not belong to Africa any more than ancient Greek art belongs to Greece. Both now belong to the world, and both are more appreciated and, above all, more fruitful

---

[85] Fagg, *Traditional Art*, p. 35, 'Tribal Sculpture', pp. 700–1.
[86] Frobenius, *Und Afrika sprach*, vol. I, p. 301. On Benin, Phillips, *Loot*.

of inspiration for the artists of today and tomorrow outside their countries than within them'.[87] By then, of course, much of both African and Greek art also belonged, in a more immediate sense, to the British Museum.

4.2 Dividing Cultures

The concept of 'culture', which the Fagg brothers used to describe the Nok, was and is central to the question of belonging. The concept was no innovation of the twentieth century. During the early modern period, the word described husbandry and gardening, as in the cultivation of land, but also the care of mind and manners. Enlightenment historians used it to differentiate between degrees of development. During the 1760s, the German clergyman Johann Gottfried Herder gave the word new meaning, closer to how we use it today. He claimed that the world had seen many different cultures, which each had their time and place. They were historically developed and not commensurable with one another. Herder first proposed this definition in a discussion about antiquities. The Halle professor Christian Adolph Klotz had employed the tools of antiquarianism to reconnect with the pagan world of antiquity and to challenge Christian morality. The ancients, Herder responded, belonged to a different culture, which could not be revived in modern Germany.[88] The antiquarian assumption, that antiquities offered an immediate connection to the past, was wrong.

During the nineteenth century, the concept became omnipresent in German scholarship. It also entered ethnology. Adolf Bastian, like others, divided the world between 'people of culture' and 'people of nature', to distinguish between those who participated in historical development and those whose life remained determined by their natural environment. However, he argued that everyone had a potential for development. The 'people of nature' were now disappearing and all that remained were some Amerindians, living in forests, people on isolated Pacific islands, and sub-Saharan Africans, who despite short 'peaks of culture' always had returned to nature.[89] Frobenius, the later explorer of Ile-Ife, further challenged the distinction. In *The Origin of African Cultures*, published in 1898, he not only insisted that Africans had culture, but also proposed an alternative way to interpret their history. The continent, he claimed, was divided geographically in 'cultural areas', revealing past migrations and influences. These areas were organic wholes, consisting not only of materials

---

[87] Fagg, 'Tribality', p. 107. On museums in Nigeria, Hellmann, *Making*. On museums in other British colonies, Mackenzie, *Museums*, and Longair and McAleer (eds.), *Curating Empire*. On the battle for restitution, Savoy, *Afrikas Kampf*. On the festival, Murphy, *First World Festival*.
[88] Eskildsen, *Modern Historiography*, pp. 57–74.
[89] Bastian, *Beiträge*, pp. ii, xiv. Also, on the concept of culture, Kroeber and Kluckhorn, *Culture*.

but also of ways of living and thinking. Understanding them demanded more than just museum collections:

> The scraps and junk that make up parts of the ethnographic collections are in themselves quite worthless. Their value lies in the fact that they are evidence of a living history of development. They are nothing but external characteristics, dead masses into which living breath needs to be blown.[90]

Curators at Ethnographic Museum in Berlin applied Frobenius' framework of 'cultural areas' to the large and recent collections from German colonies in Africa and the South Pacific. Frobenius appreciated the effort but also commented that reorganizing the collections was not enough. They needed to grasp, he remarked, 'the inner, organic, living connection'. In the anglophone world, Franz Boas, who trained at the Ethnographic Museum in Berlin but immigrated to the United States in 1886, promoted this contextual concept of culture. For the study of the past, including the recent past of 'vanishing tribes', Boas confirmed in 1907, objects remained 'the basis of studies which, without them, would be impossible'. However, their full meaning was only apparent within their context. The pipe of a North American Indian, he argued, 'is not only a curious implement out of which the Indian smokes, but it has a great number of uses and meanings, which can be understood only when viewed from the standpoint of social and religious life of the people'. This cultural critique did not stop museums from collecting. It may even have increased the yearning for things. If the objects no longer offered immediate contact to the past by themselves, they gained new meaning together with other objects from the same context. So, more artefacts, from all parts of the planet, were needed. The aim, the Berlin curator Bernhard Ankermann explained in 1914, was no longer just to collect 'show pieces', illustrating historical development, but to establish 'an inventory of the entire cultural heritage'.[91]

German archives also turned towards contextual understanding, fuelling the yearning of historians for documents. During the last decades of the nineteenth century, the so-called 'principle of provenance' was applied to the State Archives in Berlin. According to the principle, documents must remain together with other documents, produced by the same administrative units. All documents were part of historical reality and explained one another. The historian Friedrich Meinecke, who worked at the archives, described how the principle

---

[90] Frobenius, *Ursprung*, p. ix.
[91] Gräbner, 'Kulturkreise'; Ankermann, 'Kulturkreise'; Frobenius' comment, p. 89; Boas, 'Some Principles', pp. 930, 298; Ankermann, *Anleitung*, p. 9. On German museums, Penny, *Objects*, pp. 163–214; *Humboldt's Shadow*, pp. 108–11; 'Bastian's Museum'; Marchand, 'Priests'. On Boas, Jacknis, 'Ethnographic Object'.

'suddenly brought an unbelievable amount of liveliness and individuality into the entire archive. For every single administrative registry ... was now a living being with its own principle of life'. The reorganized archive revealed 'unified historical life'. The loss of any document, no matter how insignificant, endangered this unity. The yearning for things of the past knew no limits. The 'principle of provenance' was also soon exported. A prominent advocate was the historian John Franklin Jameson, who helped establish the National Archives in the United States.[92]

4.3 Dividing Tribes

German ethnologists, most importantly Eckart von Sydow, also applied the concept of 'cultural areas' to African art, with each area subdivided between ethnic groups or 'tribes'. The areas had similar characteristics, such as masques, secret societies, and 'fetish' worship in West Africa, all encouraging the production of art, but there were considerable stylistic variations within. Sydow mapped out these variations, focusing on minute differences in figurative art. In the 1930s, the Danish collector Carl Kjersmeier provided a comprehensive and illustrated overview of African 'style centres', in a geographical order and subdivided according to tribes. William Fagg was familiar with these works and adopted a similar approach at the British Museum. In 1947, Fagg reported to Kjersmeier that he 'during the past year separated all our African art specimens from the purely ethnographical pieces, and have reclassified them by tribes, instead of by colonies'. Even if this was still not reflected in the exhibits.[93]

The work in the storerooms continued for more than a decade. Curators reorganized all the ethnographic collections, and not just works of art, following Fagg's model (Figure 13). In 1956, the Keeper of Ethnography, Adrian Digby, reported that the African collections had been regrouped 'on a tribal and geographical basis'. The collections would now be sorted 'on a typological basis within the tribal groups'. Similar work with 'geographical classification' would continue in the other sections. The next year, he reported that the work with the African collections was in its 'final phase of sorting' and 'a start has been made on the geographical regrouping of the Oceanic, Asiatic and American collections'. In 1959, he presented an elaborate card system, where all ethnographic objects were divided first with red 'Political, Geographical, and

---

[92] Meinecke, *Erlebtes*, p. 142. Also, Eskildsen, 'Inventing', and, on the archival obsession, Wimmer, *Archivkörper*.

[93] Sydow, *Handbuch*; Kjersmeier, *Centres*, MS W. Fagg to C. Kjersmeier, 24 June 1947, Carl Kjersmeier. Efterladte papirer, Box 3. KB. Also, Kasfir, 'One Tribe'; Probst, *African Art*, pp. 69–71, 77.

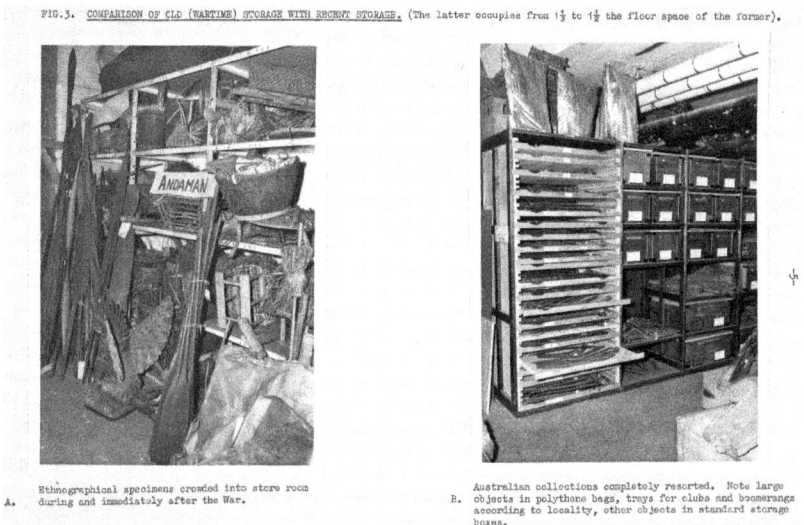

Figure 13 Comparison of old and new ordering of the storerooms from Adrian Digby's annual report, April 1960. The objects on the photo to the right are sorted first geographically, between different regions in Australia, and then typologically, with categories such as ornaments, clothing, painted belts, crafts, wooden hand clubs, baskets, and fishing nets. Courtesy The Trustees of the British Museum, United Kingdom.

Cultural area cards' and then, when possible, with ochre 'Tribal unit category guide cards'. So, the categories were applied to all objects and to people from all over in the world.[94]

Fagg's initial purpose was to enlarge European comprehension of African cultures. In 1951, in the catalogue for the exhibition at the Imperial Institute in London, he briefly discussed the divide separating the visitors from the sculptures. Europeans, he claimed, were bound by mental habits, inherited from the ancient Greeks and developed in the Renaissance, which prioritized the scientific reproduction of nature. African art, on the contrary, was poetic, emphasizing analogy, metaphor, and symbolism. Most Europeans were not able to appreciate this art and wrongfully dismissed it as 'primitive'. They needed the helping hand of 'anthropologists specializing in material culture', who worked on 'tribal cultures' and had developed tools for 'the analytical study of tribal art forms'.[95]

---

[94] MS A. Digby, Department of Ethnography, Minutes of the Meeting, Sub-Committee on Antiquities, etc., June 1, 1956, p. 5, July 9, 1957, p. 1, 4, June 10, 1959, pp. 10–12, CA, BM. Also, Grout, *Museum Correspondences*, pp. 206–8.

[95] Fagg, *Traditional Art*, p. 7.

A similar interest in translating between European and African concepts of art informed his other early works.

As the British colonies in West Africa gained independence, during the late 1950s and early 1960s, Fagg became more concerned about the understanding of Africans. The British Empire had introduced a system of 'indirect rule', employing and enforcing ethnic divisions. According to Fagg, this had ensured the survival of traditions and the protection of the art and craftsmanship. British administrators, traders, and missionaries had also not, like their continental counterparts, emptied their colonies for artefacts. Those in Nigeria, he explained in 1963, 'were rarely collectors', and 'never from commercial motives', but had instead developed 'the best museum service in Africa'. He acknowledged the so-called 'Punitive Expedition' to Benin in 1897, which looted thousands of artefacts. However, he merely described it as an 'historical accident' ensuring 'that African art suddenly acquired a real presence in the civilized world'. African art was now exhibited in European and North American museums and profoundly influenced contemporary artists.[96] Contemporary Africans, he claimed, did not have a similar appreciation.

4.4 Dividing Past and Present

Fagg's changing views on Africans' relationship to their past may have been informed by his collaboration with art dealers and collectors. This collaboration intensified after independence, which made fieldwork and acquisitions in Africa difficult. The private market for world art, as discussed in Section 3, emerged during the nineteenth century. Vendors also sold artefacts from European colonies in Africa. The demand exploded during the first decades of the twentieth century, when artists, such as Derain, Picasso, Matisse, and Modigliani, found inspiration in African art, and it was sold together with their works in galleries in Paris and New York. During this period, claims about the high antiquity of African art served both as legitimation and as a marketing tool. The poet Guillaume Apollinaire described African art as an older inspiration to ancient Egyptian art and the critic Félix Fénéon advocated that it belonged in the Louvre, together with other great historical traditions. The prominent art dealer Paul Guillaume postulated that wooden sculptures, sold in his gallery in Paris, were many centuries old.[97]

By the mid twentieth century, however, scholars, dealers, and collectors alike agreed that most of these works, especially those made in wood, were

---

[96] Fagg, *Nigerian Images*, pp. 19–20.
[97] On the problems with acquisition, Grout, *Museum Correspondences*, pp. 160–70. On the African art market. Biro, *Fabriquer*; Monroe; *Metropolitan Fetish*, pp. 49–83, 112–22.

relatively recent. Historical artefacts from before the nineteenth century were in limited supply. Those that showed up on the market, such as the remains of the loot from Benin, were getting exceedingly expensive. The contextual concept of culture offered a solution. Charles Ratton, who replaced Paul Guillaume as the dominant force on the Parisian African art market during the 1930s, prepared the way for this approach. Unlike Guillaume, he was familiar with contemporary ethnographic research and collaborated with major museums, especially the Ethnographic Museum at the Trocadéro in Paris. As early as 1931, Ratton published an essay arguing that African art represented an entirely different 'mentality' and 'millennia old, animist ideas'. One of the 'essential characteristics' of this world was 'its integrity, its impermeability to external influences'. This old unchangeable order, however, had disappeared 'at the moment' when Europeans appeared and 'there is no more black art'. So, the artefacts may not be very old but, nonetheless, were things of the past, revealing an entirely different historical world beyond. From the late 1940s, Ratton closely collaborated with Fagg, meeting regularly and contributing with artefacts from his private collection to exhibitions and written works. Fagg republished this 1931 essay as introduction to one of his books as late as 1980.[98]

During the 1960s, Fagg connected the division between past and present to the variations among African tribes, which he had studied in the storage rooms of the British Museum since the 1940s. Africans, he emphasized, were not only distinct from Europeans, but also, through their different cultures and religions, from one another. In 1963, he introduced the concept of 'Tribality' to explain these distinctions. In 1965, he published *Tribes and Forms in African Art*, overviewing over a hundred African tribes, each represented by one artefact, illustrating 'the separateness of tribal styles'. European artists, collectors, and curators now understood the universality of art, but, he claimed, Africans did not: 'All these arts form a single universe *for us*; but they do not form a single universe absolutely. On the contrary, when we examine the tribal arts in themselves, we find that every tribe is, from the point of view of art, a universe to itself'. Tribes were dynamic, sometimes shared characteristics, and there were areas where artistic frontiers were open. But Fagg nonetheless insisted that 'the sculpture of one tribe will be meaningless and unintelligible to people in another tribe'. The 'blockage' between tribes, he claimed a few years

---

[98] Ratton, *Masques africains*, unpag, republished in Fagg, *Masques*, pp. 7–12, many letters between C. Ratton and W. Fagg, from 1949 to 1975, William Buller Fagg Papers, RAI. On Benin bronzes, Bodenstein, 'Notes'. On Ratton, Monroe, *Metropolitan Fetish*, pp. 174–234; Dagen, *Charles Ratton*.

later, had enabled 'Africa to develop thousands of separate styles during the same period when Europe was developing one'.[99]

Fagg's tribal distinctions were geographical rather than historical. His *Tribes and Forms* opened with a map of Africa with tribes marked in different areas. The artworks were presented from West to East. Even the Nok, Fagg introduced geographically, between a wooden Afo stool, collected in 1904, and undated Mama buffalo mask, in Ratton's collection. However, unlike other contemporary surveys, Fagg described tribal arts as dead or dying. In French and Belgian colonies, he claimed, the arts were almost gone. In Nigeria, they were now disappearing. So, the geographical order did not exist anymore and, he explained, a proper map 'would need to be drawn as at a date such as 1900 or 1918, so heavy has been the erosion of African art since then by the processes of social and material decay and of commerce'. This situation was only made worse by the new African elites, preoccupied with 'nationalism' and *négritude*, imports from Europe that had 'no roots in Africa'. The 'Gods' of African art, he concluded in 1976, 'have lost their strength and cannot withstand civilization, or independent governments'. It was a 'long farewell', with some still holding on to their tribal cultures, but a farewell nonetheless.[100]

These ideas informed Fagg's lecture, entitled 'Tribality', at First World Festival of Negro Arts, in Dakar, in 1966. His claim that the African art 'does not belong to Africa' was based not only on the new European appreciation but also on the diversity and disappearance of tribal cultures. Their diversity prevented tribal Africans from appreciating the arts of other tribes. Modern 'detribalized' Africans, especially among the intellectual elites, were alienated from their past and its arts. And tribal art was 'moribund' and 'the art of the past'. Once, he explained, he had believed that all Africans had a deeper 'intuitive understanding' of African art than Europeans. Now, he realized that this assumption was wrong.[101]

4.5 Selling the Things of the Past

Fagg retired from the British Museum in 1974 and instead joined the London auction house Christie's. His views on tribal art, developed as a curator, informed his approach as a vendor. Christie's catalogues, published during his tenure from 1974 to 1990, sometimes added longer descriptions. This could be for rare, old, or expensive objects, such as Benin bronzes, or because of

---

[99] Fagg, *Tribes and Forms*, pp. 9–13. Emphasis in the original. *Miniature Wood Carvings*, p. 10. First use of 'Tribality' in *Nigerian Images*, p. 79.
[100] Fagg, *Tribes and Forms*, p. 13; *African Sculpture*, p. 7; 'Long Farewell', p. 23. Also, 'Tribality and Post-Tribality'. On tribal art as a living tradition, Probst, *African Art*, pp. 79–82, 87–108.
[101] Fagg, 'Tribality', pp. 107, 108, 110.

extraordinary beauty or curious tribal significance. Another common reason was provenance. Ratton started mentioning provenance in the 1930s as a marketing strategy. The artists were mostly unknown, so he instead associated the works with distinguished collectors, whose tastes were beyond doubt. This also occasionally happened in the Christie's catalogues. However, the provenance was usually linked to colonial administrators, soldiers, or sailors, who were not known for their aesthetic sensibilities. It did not guarantee taste, but instead that objects were collected in Africa before the demise of tribal cultures, usually before 1930.[102]

The catalogues also noted differences between artefacts for sale and later corruptions. The artefacts in the salesroom represented vanished tribal cultures, and this ensured their historical, aesthetic, and monetary value. Later artefacts, which no longer represented these cultures, had been excluded. Because of the 'long farewell', the time of the temporal break varied. In Congo, Luba Kifwebe masks remained tribal and there was no 'mass-production' until World War II. The Songye Kifwebe masks, on the contrary, experienced 'a wide measure of stereotyping' during the 1930s as 'the tourists increased' and 'all those which had individual merit had been made long before'. The Kuyu also 'descended into complete banality about 1930'. The problem was not just a decline in craftsmanship, but also that Africans, through the encounter with the outside world, became self-aware and consequently stopped producing authentic artefacts. For another Congo group, the Kuba, Fagg dated the transition from tribal to tourist art exactly to 1913, when the gift of a royal statue to a European unleashed 'the great climacteric which marks the appearance of "feedback" and selfconsciousness in Kuba art'.[103]

Many entries mentioned that 'William Fagg' had seen or photographed something similar during his trips to Africa. In one catalogue, he even offered a short description of his early career at the British Museum and his fieldwork among Nigerian wood carvers. So, his long personal experience as a curator, going back to the 1940s, restored the connection between vanished tribal cultures and the surviving objects in the salesroom. The fieldwork also confirmed the temporal break between the artefacts for sale and later corruptions. A Yoruba carver, named Bamgboye, personally embodied the break. The carver was given a job at a government school 'about 1930' and this 'had the unforeseen effect of "turning him off" by making him self-conscious'. One artefact

---

[102] The following is based on Christie's tribal art catalogues in Fagg's private library at RAI. For a selection, Fagg, *One Hundred Notes*. On Fagg and Christie's, Waterfield, 'Working'. On provenance, Monroe, 'Market'.

[103] Christie's catalogues, RAI, 22 June 1981, p. 51, 28 November 1984, p. 65, 28 November 1982, p. 58, 17 June 1980, p. 53.

resembled the 'house style' of the carver Laleye Labode, whom Fagg had meet, but it was, he noted, 'very much superior to Laleye's work and must have been from the previous generation'.[104]

Most artists discussed were active before 1930. They were often not named but described just as 'master carver' or given pseudonyms, such as 'the Master of the Archaic Smile' or 'the Master of the Uneven Eyes'. A few exceptions were made for more recent pieces, such as a pair of ibeji, representing dead twins, by the carver Dada, known as Areogun, sold in 1980. Fagg mentioned that both he and another visitor had photographed an 'exactly similar' work 'being held by its living twin sister, named Taiwo' (Figure 14). So, his photo,

Figure 14 Taiwo with her twin ibeji by Dada, known as Areogun, in Osi, Nigeria. Photo by William Fagg, 1959. Courtesy Royal Anthropological Institute, United Kingdom.

---

[104] Ibid., 24 June 1985, pp. 61–2. 13 October 1978, p. 39. Also, 31 March 1982, p. 20. 22 June 1981, p. 45.

taken in 1959 shortly before Nigerian independence, proved that Areogun had produced for a tribal culture, which, regular readers of Fagg's books and Christie's catalogues would know, now had disappeared. It turned the figures for sale into things of the past, remains of a lost historical world, although they were close to contemporary. This transformation was possible because the figure on the photo was not a thing of the past, but living reality, to Taiwo.[105]

4.6 Reclaiming the Past

Africans also contributed to the discussions. At the colloquium in Dakar in 1966, Fagg mentioned that there in 'the field of art and antiquities' was 'only one person (a member of this Colloquium) who has reached the necessary academic standard in the whole of Anglophone Africa'. He was referring to Ekpo Eyo, who had briefly worked at the British Museum and here participated in the reorganization of the ethnographic storage rooms. He later became the first native Nigerian to serve as director of the Nigerian Department of Antiquities. At the colloquium, Eyo subtly criticized his former mentor. The universal appreciation of African arts, which Fagg now praised and promoted, he presented as a problem. The 'awareness of the beauty of African art in Europe and America', Eyo argued, 'has drained the African Continent of most of what is left over by white ants and other factors. Right from the time of the Punitive Expedition to Benin in 1897 and the visit of Leo Frobenius, Europeans and Americans have not ceased to collect whatever African works of art that come their way'. This was especially a problem for historical understanding. Where 'written historical records are rare or only recent', the artefacts were the only way to the past.[106]

African arts and crafts did not belong in a different unchangeable order, together with ethnographic objects from around the world, but proved changes over time. Scholars therefore should approach them like they long had approached European antiquities. Eyo's most significant publication *Two thousand years Nigerian Art*, from 1977, was a manifesto for the historical understanding of African art. The book repeatedly criticized interpretations that denied historical development. Understanding history, in its diversity, Eyo argued, demanded that scholars abandoned ideas of 'primitive' art, which placed African art at some imaginary beginning. It also demanded a revision of the concept of 'tribality'. It was plainly wrong, he insisted, that Africans could not understand or appreciate one another's art. Throughout history, they had exchanged artistic ideas as well as objects. This could be proven from the artefacts themselves as well as from where they were found.

---

[105] Ibid., 28 November 1984, p. 21, 15 March 1978, p. 33, 17 June 1980, p. 23.
[106] Fagg, 'Tribality', p. 111; Eyo, 'Preservation', pp. 580, 577. Identification of the one scholar, MS W. Fagg to Dr. Thomas, 15 April 1975, William Buller Fagg Papers, RAI. On Eyo and the British Museum, Grout, *Museum Correspondences*, pp. 205–20.

Ethnographic observations proved a similar interplay. Africans often used objects from other ethnic groups, and wood carvers and traditional doctors served several groups. It was, he concluded his book, a 'false premise that cultures are stagnant, that they should be encapsulated and preserved from external influences'. These ideas also influenced his curatorial practices. At the Nigerian National Museum in Lagos, he arranged exhibitions 'to cut across ethnic divisions as to bring out the cultural inter-relationships of the peoples of Nigeria'.[107]

Eyo was not only critical of the division between tribes but also rejected the idea that African arts and crafts only belonged in the past. Colonialism had been disruptive, especially in Benin, but artists and craftsmen continued evolving. At the museum, he presented arts and crafts as living traditions and highlighted innovations, changes in styles, and uses of new materials. In the guidebook, he noted that the objects had varying purposes as well. In connection to the wood carvings of Bamgboye and Areogun, he mentioned that such human figures 'may have no more significance than a child's plaything. Or they may be carried in dances simply in order to attract attention'. Sometimes they were used for decoration 'without having any particular religious significance'. This emphasis on renewal and reinterpretation also informed the purpose of the museum. Like the European and Japanese museums discussed in Section 1, Nigerian museums should not only preserve and present the past but also motivate contemporaries 'by showing actual objects which are the products of man's skill and inventiveness'. The artefacts, Eyo argued, should 'act as an inspiration for the evolution of new forms and norms'. This inspiration was especially necessary in a time, where 'we have come to the end of an era in our traditional crafts, and that new art forms have to develop'.[108]

4.7 Reclaiming the Things of the Past

Learning from 'actual objects' was only possible if the artefacts were in Nigeria. From the late 1960s, Eyo joined the chorus of African leaders and intellectuals demanding restitution from colonial powers and became one of the loudest voices on the continent. This work for restitution was closely connected to his curatorial work. In 1977, he helped prepare the second World Black and African Festival of Arts and Culture, following the one in Dakar in 1966. He also curated an exhibit on Nigerian art, which inspired his larger book, published the same year. He contacted museums around the world to borrow artefacts for the exhibit and was especially interested in the famous ivory mask of Queen Idia from Benin, which after 1897

---

[107] Eyo, *Two Thousand Years*, p. 216; 'Nigerian National Museum', p. 5.
[108] Ibid., p. 6; *Two Thousand Years*, pp. 220, 218; *Guide*, p. 38. Also, on his curatorial practices, 'Different Methods'.

had ended up at the British Museum. The museum declined. The refusal, Eyo later argued, illustrated the emptiness of arguments about the universality of museums, and revealed a reality where 'art treasures flow in from the "peripheries of the world" to the "centre" and not from the "centre" outwards'.[109]

In 1980, he curated the first large exhibit of art from Nigerian museums to tour abroad, in the United States and several European countries. The exhibition, 'Treasures of Ancient Nigeria', only included artefacts from before the twentieth century, proving the long history of art, starting with the Nok figures, as well as pointing to the disruptive consequences of colonialism. In the catalogue, he also discussed the catastrophe in 1897, which 'effectively brought an end to traditional Benin art', and concluded:

> Benin is now left to show remnants and second-rate objects, as well as casts and photographs of pieces that once belonged to them. Perhaps it is time that the circumstances in which these objects were removed from Benin should be looked at again. Museums that have acquired the works of art could lend one object, maybe two, and if these are collected from several sources, perhaps Benin Museum itself would be able to show Benin works in their proper context.[110]

The 'proper context' of Benin artefacts was not just together with other Benin artefacts. If so, they should stay in London and Berlin. It was instead in the original context of Benin City. In an interview with the *New York Times*, in connection with the tour of the exhibition, Eyo again advocated for restitution and critiqued arguments about the universality of art. A Benin head, he insisted, 'represents a particular oba, or king, was not meant to be an art piece, it was spiritual, it was political ... The aesthetic side was only secondary. So it would have more meaning among the people who made it than among people who just see it as an art piece'. As things of the past, the remains had a different purpose in the present.[111]

Again, the campaign did not result in returns. A few years later, Eyo even speculated that the exhibition, and the ensuing interest in Nigerian art, had encouraged illicit traffic and theft from Nigerian museums. These experiences also sensitized Eyo to problems with the art trade. At a seminar at the California Institute of Technology in 1981, Eyo returned to his critique of Fagg's concept of 'tribality' and added a note about the role of the words, 'primitive' and 'tribal', on the art market. Some academics now rejected these words but, he noted, this did not discourage art dealers: 'Take a walk down Park, Fifth, or

---

[109] Eyo, 'Threat', p. 203. Also, on Eyo's work for restitution, Savoy, *Afrikas Kampf*, pp. 11–20, 25–44, 89–92, and, on the mask, Bodenstein, 'Diplomatie'; Malaquais and Vincent, 'Three Takes'.
[110] Eyo, *Treasures*, pp. 18–19.   [111] Fraser, 'New Insight', p. 70.

Madison Avenues in New York and you will find numerous art galleries dedicated to the sale of "primitive" or "tribal" art. Go to London, where in the two famous art sale rooms, Sotheby's and Christie's, one has a department of primitive art and the other of tribal art'. The latter, of course, was Fagg's invention as well.[112]

4.8 Escape from History?

The culmination of European colonialism, during the late nineteenth and early twentieth centuries, coincided with the culmination of the modern yearning for things of the past. Europeans amassed large amounts of artefacts from conquered territories to fill their museums. These museums served colonial interests but also pursued scholarly goals. The dream of writing a new world history or mapping out different 'cultural areas' or 'tribal cultures' had consequences around the world. From the late nineteenth century, the art market accelerated this process and contributed to the global redistribution of historical artefacts. Some countries established large museums and plentiful private collections. Other countries lost many of their antiquities and acquired few artefacts from other parts of world.

This redistribution changed the relationship between past and present. The removal of objects not only disrupted traditions but also delegitimized renewal. Ratton in Paris and Fagg in London established a temporal boundary, coinciding with colonialism, between an African past and a non-African present. Africa no longer produced artefacts, like those in the storage of British Museum, and therefore appeared to be empty. As Fagg put it bluntly in 1975: 'When tribal art dies out in an area, what replaces it? The answer is a vacuum.' The relationship also changed in countries of origin. The anthropologist Christopher Steiner did fieldwork among art traders in Côte d'Ivoire during the late 1980s and early 1990s. He noted that their concept of authenticity differed from that of European dealers and collectors. In Abidjan, tribal cultures did not make artefacts authentic, but European museums and collections did instead. Those artefacts still in circulation in Africa, according to the traders, were only copies.[113]

Many scholars, not only in Africa, but also in Europe and North America, have since criticized the division between past and present. The Museum of Modern Art in New York in 1984 opened a large exhibition on 'Primitivism'. The cultural critic James Clifford wrote a scolding commentary. The museum,

---

[112] Eyo, 'Primitivism', p. 19. On illicit trade, 'Threat', pp. 204–11. On Fagg and the tribal arts department at Christie's, Waterfield, 'Working'.
[113] Fagg, 'Tribality and Post-Tribality', unpag. Steiner, *African Art*, pp. 100–3.

together with the American Museum of Natural History, sustained 'aesthetic-anthropological object systems', which transformed tribal arts into 'something located in the past, good for being collected and given aesthetic value'. The exhibitions were products of curatorial choices, which hid colonial legacies and denied intercultural dialogue and development. This approach, he also noted, was now being challenged. Other museums in New York, collaborating with people from countries of origin, showed vibrant and living traditions. Clifford emphasized a recent exhibition on 'Igbo Arts' at the Center for African Art, co-curated by the Igbo scholar and artist Chike Aniakor and with numerous artefacts borrowed from Eyo's Nigerian National Museum in Lagos. Instead of dividing, Clifford argued, the exhibit showed 'past *and* present heritage'.[114]

Despite such critiques and challenges, the division is still enforced in museums and especially on the art market. Christie's and Sotheby's have renamed their departments dealing with African arts to more neutral geographical names, but collectors remain obsessed with tribal arts. Their preference is African arts, which make up around half of sold tribal art lots and most of the revenue. Ever higher prices are paid for exceptional artefacts, from or before the colonial period. Jean-Baptiste Bacquart's *The Tribal Arts of Africa*, written while he worked at Sotheby's during the 1990s, has now replaced Fagg's books as standard reference work. Like his predecessor, Bacquart orders objects geographically and not historically, but, nonetheless, separates the past from the present. The newest objects are 'from the beginning of the 20th century, before the commercialization of tribal art for the tourist trade'. Connections to tribal cultures ensure their authenticity. For artefacts to be 'genuine', they 'must have been used during tribal ceremonies'.[115]

The division between past and present may reflect actual changes, resulting from colonialism and trade, and genuine aesthetic preferences. However, as already Eyo pointed out, the division is detrimental not only to the development of arts and crafts, but also to historical understanding. It can only be maintained, with Clifford's words, through a 'distortion', where 'history has been airbrushed out'.[116] History disappears in the past, which is reduced to an unchangeable order. History also disappears in the present, which, to those believing, no longer produces artefacts worth noticing. The division, simultaneously, pretends to be historical and prevents historical interpretation. Over the centuries, historical scholarship has constantly expanded its realm and considered ever more and

---

[114] Clifford, *Predicament*, pp. 189–214, quotes on pp. 209, 206, 207. Emphasis in the original. For the exhibition on Igbo arts, Cole, *Igbo Arts*.
[115] Bacquart, *Tribal Arts*, p. 9. For a discussion of a recent museum, the Musée du quai Branly in Paris, Price, *Paris Primitive*. On market trends, Thibault, *Tribal Art Market*.
[116] Clifford, *Predicament*, p. 202.

more diverse artefacts. The antiquarian investigations of the ruins of Rome expanded to monuments on other continents. Scholars widened the scope of the history of art from Greek and Roman antiquity to all people on earth and supplemented with histories of technology and craftsmanship. Recent history attracted interest. Everywhere, the investigations have uncovered differences and changes over time. Those interested in the African past, of course, have found differences and changes in Africa as well.[117] There are, as argued in the next section, no necessary limits to historical scholarship. Things turn into things of the past when we use them to connect with the past. No part of the world was ever empty.

5 Many Things

5.1 The Kodama and Gotō Statues

The oldest museum in Taiwan is housed in a neoclassical building, with a Greek temple façade and Doric and Corinthian columns, next to a park in the centre of Taipei. The museum opened in 1915, during Japanese occupation, as a colonial museum. Its official name was Memorial Hall for Kodama and Gotō. When entering visitors would see two life-size bronze statues of the Governor-General Kodama Gentarō and Civil Administrator Gotō Shinpei, placed in elevated alcoves in the central rotunda of the museum. After taking over in 1945, the Chinese nationalist government of Chiang Kai-shek worked hard to erase the memory of the Japanese. The museum was renamed Taiwan Provincial Museum, and the statues were put in storage. The museum changed names again in 2003 to National Taiwan Museum. The statues returned to public view in 2008, but not to their former prominent venue. They are now shown in a humbler room on the third floor (Figure 15).[118] An adjacent permanent exhibition, 'Discovering Taiwan', which opened in 2017, explains the early history of the museum as well as the work of Japanese scholars on the archaeological, cultural, and natural history of the Island.

National Taiwan Museum presents a Taiwanese history that is different from that of China and includes half a century as a Japanese colony. This message has political significance at a time when China challenges Taiwan's right to self-rule. However, the museum not just invents a history, as the nationalist government did when it demolished Shinto temples and instead plastered Taipei with grandiose buildings in northern Chinese palace style. It presents a history, accessible through material remains, previously hidden away in the storage rooms. Such findings can happen all over the world. The National Historical Museum of Brazil in 2009 made a new exhibit about the age of exploration,

---

[117] For a recent historical overview of African art history, Blier, *History*. Also, on the history of African art history, Probst, *African Art*.

[118] Allan, *Taipei*, pp. 117–20.

Figure 15 Bronze statues of Gotō Shinpei and Kodama Gentarō, by the Japanese sculptor Taketarō Shinkai, on the third floor of the National Taiwan Museum. The plaque in the middle once hung above the museum's entrance. Photo by Kasper Risbjerg Eskildsen, 2023. Courtesy National Taiwan Museum.

'Portuguese in the World'. Among the objects was a wooden statue, described as a fertility goddess, representing Africa (Figure 16). Later, curators realized that the statue had belonged to the Brotherhood of Our Lady of the Blacks of Ouro Preto, Brazil. It had been mislabelled and forgotten for half a century in the storage rooms. In 2022, the statue, while remaining in the exhibit, received a new description as the 'Maria Cambinda' and served as the centre piece in a rethinking of the museum, foregrounding the Brazilian black communities and intercultural dialogue across the Atlantic.[119]

The exhibitions at the National Taiwan Museum and the National Historical Museum of Brazil illustrate how the engagement with things of the past has become a global phenomenon. Uncovering the past through things is no longer the privilege of a few European scholars, but a possibility everywhere. This global interest in artefacts is not necessarily an expression of 'nationalist' agendas, insisting on similarities between past and present, as sometimes claimed in the museum debates about acquisition and restitution. It is unlikely that the Taiwanese, who now engage with the remains of their Japanese past,

---

[119] Magalhães and Plazzi, 'Maria Cambinda', 'Brasil decolonial'.

Figure 16 Carved wooden sculpture/mask, called 'Maria Cambinda' (110 x 21 cm), from around 1850. Unknown artist. Photo by Jaime Acioli. Courtesy Museu Histórico Nacional/Ibram, Brazil.[120]

dream of returning to colonialism. The recovery of their material history, however, proves that Taiwan has been organized in many ways and that many people and cultures contributed. It allows them to imagine change and supports the development of Taiwan's pluralistic democracy. Similarly, the Brazilian recasting of the Maria Cambinda is not aimed at reviving old rituals. The museum instead portrays Brazil's diverse history, with influences from different parts of the world, to imagine a more inclusive society. The engagement with historical differences also serves a purpose in the present.[121]

'Universal' or 'encyclopaedic' museums, gathering objects from many parts of the world, have also become a global attraction. Every year, millions of people travel to see the famous museums in European capitals. Many countries

---

[120] Public domain. No. 004046
[121] For the 'nationalist' accusation, Cuno, *Who Owns*. On African history at the National Historical Museum of Brazil, Magalhães, 'diáspora africana'.

outside of Europe now have museums with universal ambitions. During the first half of the nineteenth century, the Brazilian imperial family started buying up European and Egyptian artefacts for their museum, later the National Museum of Brazil, which tragically burned down in 2018. The two first such museums in North America were the Museum of Fine Arts in Boston and the Metropolitan Museum in New York, both founded in 1870. The CSMVS in Mumbai, then the Prince of Wales Museum of Western India, opened in 1922, at the bequest of local citizens and with donations from the Tata family. Today, variations can be found around the world, including museums for other 'civilizations', Asian Civilizations Museum in Singapore, Museum of Islamic Civilization in Sharjah, and Museum of Black Civilizations in Dakar, which opened in 1997, 2008, and 2018, and a franchise of an older European museum, Louvre Abu Dhabi, established in 2017.[122] These developments, of course, do not mean that the artefacts now are accessible to everyone. The tourists flocking to museums belong to a small global elite. In much of the world, museums primarily contain local artefacts. The problems with unequal distribution, discussed in Section 4, have not been solved. However, 'universal' or 'encyclopaedic' museums are no longer just a European obsession. The injustice of unequal distribution seems to be less of an issue to countries, which have acquired the resources to establish such museums.

5.2 Many Ways to Things

The Taiwanese and Brazilian engagement with material history also shows how all things potentially can become things of the past. It doesn't matter whether these things are everyday items, religious icons, or reminders of a brutal colonial past. All things are, if nothing else, remains of their creation. They offer testimony to this situation, which informs historical scholarship. When transformed into the things of the past, they change meaning. In 1915, when the bronze statues of Kodame and Gotō were placed in the rotunda of the new museum in Taipei, they represented colonial power. In Brazil, the Maria Cambinda was originally a religious icon, used in processions. In their historicized contexts, the figures instead become remains of forgotten and suppressed parts of history and, as such, grain immediate relevance in present-day Taiwan and Brazil.

This transformation can even happen to fakes. Since the fifteenth century, among those yearning for things of the past, nothing has been more hated than forgers and forgeries. To those longing for confirmation, and similarities between past and present, reproductions are not necessarily a problem. They

---

[122] Also, Grau, *Under Discussion*.

already know what they want to find. Some, like the Chinese nationalist government after its arrival in Taiwan, invent the heritage that they need. To those, on the contrary, who want to uncover differences, reproductions are the ultimate deceit, promising access but not delivering. However, deceitful objects are also remains of their creation. In Colombia, the Alzate ceramics, discussed in Section 3, are no longer just considered as counterfeits, but also as creative reinterpretations of the tradition, worthy of study for their own sake. They have even been interpreted as a form of indigenous revenge against the colonizers.[123] So, when the fakes are turned into things of the past, they also acquire new meanings and offer insights into histories that previously have been ignored.

While all things potentially can become things of the past, historical scholarship does not necessarily replace other ways of engaging with things. This Element started with Fenollosa's and Okakura's arrival at the Hōryūji Temple, in the summer of 1884, and uncovering of the Guze Kannon. The visit transformed the statue into a thing of the past and changed their view of Japanese art history. However, the statue remained in the temple and retained its religious meaning. The borders between different communities of meaning are often open. Ideas, objects, and persons move back and forth. The strongest case may be the relationship between antiquarianism and historical scholarship. Despite changing positions of authority, as in Japan during the 1870s and 1880s, antiquaries never disappeared. They still view artefacts in other ways than archaeologist or art historians. The oily patina, oxidized wood, and scratches on an old cabinet offer satisfaction, even if nothing is known about its situation of creation. Objects can be exhibited and enjoyed without caring about historical context and development. Over the past centuries, antiquarianism and historical scholarship have supplemented one another. Antiquaries have ensured the preservation of artefacts. Historical scholarship has informed the interests of collectors. In Colombia, as seen in Section 3, Zerda employed antiquarian collections to imagine a historical museum. In England, as discussed in Section 4, Fagg employed his experience from the British Museum as a vendor at Christie's.

Okakura also crossed these open borders. In 1904, he found employment as a curator at the Museum in Fine Arts in Boston. Soon after, he formed a close friendship with the collector Isabella Stewart Gardener. In her large private museum, a few hundred meters from the Museum of Fine Art, Gardner exhibited artefacts from different places and periods next to one another, revered in their aesthetic qualities, and emphasised their connection to her personal life-story. Okakura's most popular book, *The Book of Tea*, was written in this

---

[123] Giraldo '"A" de Alzate'. Also, on fakes and historical research, Eskildsen, 'Fälschung'.

atmosphere. In the book, he not only presented the Japanese 'Philosophy of Tea', or 'Teaism', but also reflected on different ways to appreciate things. The modern age, he complained, confused 'art with archaeology'. Collectors were 'anxious to acquire specimens to illustrate a school or period', forgetting the value of masterpieces. 'We classify too much and enjoy too little' and the 'so-called scientific method of exhibition' destroyed museums.[124] This critique, however, did not prevent Okakura from working as a curator. Antiquarian and historical approaches do not necessarily exclude one another, and both remain possible, as long as there are people interested and institutions supporting them. This is true for other approaches as well. The continuation of the Hōryūji Temple, as a Buddhist institution, and the dedication of the monks still enable the veneration of the Guze Kannon today.

Historical scholarship is also still competing with more destructive approaches to antiquities. From the fifteenth to the nineteenth century, as discussed in Section 2, European soldiers, missionaries, and colonial administrators destroyed countless artefacts considered as idols of the Devil. The global scale was unprecedented, but the iconoclasm, inspired by the ban of idolatry of the Abrahamic religions, was not new. Long before Lord Elgin, in late antiquity, Christian devotees defaced much of the artwork on the Parthenon, representing pagan gods. The iconoclasm continues today, in recent decades not least by Islamic fundamentalists in Afghanistan, Iraq, Syria, and elsewhere. To these fundamentalists, the modern obsession with antiquities appears yet another form of idol worship. The designation of ruins and monuments as World Heritage, and the public outrage when they are destroyed, just offer opportunity for media attention.[125]

5.3 Do We Need the Things?

Historical scholarship, however, did offer a new approach to antiquities. It transformed old things into things of the past. Over the last centuries, scholars have ensured that these things have become central to our sense of the past as well as of the contemporary world. This engagement with the things of the past has not been without consequences. For many, historical scholarship has been a problem. As discussed in this Element, historical scholarship has disturbed some, who cherished the religious and social order of society and found comfort in traditional ways of living and thinking. The removal of objects from temples and royal courts disrupted old rituals and habits, and ripped artefacts of their

---

[124] Okakura, *Book*, pp. 117–8.
[125] On Christian iconoclasm and the Parthenon, Rubiés, 'Theology'; Pollini, 'Christian Destruction'. On Islamic fundamentalists, Flood, 'Idol-Breaking'.

religious and symbolic significance. The historical and comparative investigations, enabled by this removal, often have been troublesome as well.

The primary problem for traditionalists may not be that historical scholarship distinguished between Europeans and non-Europeans and denied that all were equal parts of historical development. Some historical works have indeed served, what Johannes Fabian called, the 'denial of coevalness', and placed the rest of the world, with Dipesh Chakrabarty's expression, in the 'waiting room' of history.[126] Enlightenment historians and philosophers, presented in Section 2, performed such achronological operations when positioning Amerindians outside of time. Twentieth-century art dealers and museum curators, discussed in Section 4, continued when dividing the African past from the non-African present. However, these theories also suggested that modernity and diversity were incompatible and, some scholars added, that diversity may be preferable. So, the divisions also have supplied arguments in defence of tradition.

The problem for traditionalists is instead that historical scholarship promotes a peculiar vision of modernity. The work started in Europe, when scholars challenged biblical and mythical histories and questioned the religious and social order, as described in Section 2. Scholars around the world contributed as well, when disproving theories that denied their participation in historical development, as discussed in Sections 2–4. The modernizing work continues today in Taiwan and Brazil, when museum curators reorganize exhibits and present more diverse histories of their countries. Scholars don't have to ignore their findings, or compromise with academic standards and curatorial principles, to promote this vision of modernity. Doing their work, searching through archives, libraries, archaeological sites, and museum storage rooms, is enough. By revealing changes, they encourage changes. By uncovering differences, they enable differences. The past is the problem.

Even in Europe, this vision of modernity was never fully accepted. Most people engaging with old things still prefer confirmation over contingency, similarity over difference, and heritage over history. These viewpoints may be a greater challenge to historical scholarship than museum debates about acquisition and restitution. Exploring the past demands considerable efforts and resources. If governments no longer should be interested, they just could stop funding historical research. Many occupied in the business may benefit as well. Archaeological sites could attract more visitors as historical theme parks and venues for re-enactments. Museums could endear audiences and donors, emphasizing the aesthetic and emotional appeal of artefacts. Universities

---

[126] Fabian, *Time*, pp. 71–104. Chakrabarty, *Provincializing Europe*, pp. 8–10.

could prepare students better for the job market, transforming history and archaeology programs into tourism and heritage studies. These changes have been happening for decades now.[127] They have also allowed more democratic approaches to monuments and artefacts, better reflecting the interests and wishes of the public at large.

A different challenge to historical scholarship is that many do not care about the past at all. There are other visions of modernity, associated with science and technology, material wealth and development, urbanization and infrastructure, administration and bureaucracy, and law and political institutions. These visions also encourage change, often in much more dramatic ways, imagining entirely new beginnings. In comparison, the modernizing effect of historical scholarship may seem insignificant. It may even, with its emphasis upon connecting past and present, seem counterproductive. During the Cultural Revolution, from 1966 to 1976, the Chinese Communist party systematically destroyed material remains of the past. The beginning of a new area demanded the disappearance of the old.[128] Today, destruction is usually less ideological and based on financial and societal interests. In recent decades, historic neighbourhoods in China, and many other countries, have been flattened and replaced with high-rises at a rapid pace. This has enabled urbanization and better lives and living conditions for much of world's population. Why look back and obsess about the material remains? Accommodating nostalgia and the need for heritage, as now also happens in Chinese cities, development can even include new tourist sites and shopping malls, build in historical style.

So, you can imagine a world, without the things of the past. In this alternative world, some people would still collect old things, as they have done always, everywhere. There may also be museums, but, like two centuries ago, with other purposes than recovering a different past. Scholars no longer would need to roam the world, searching for material remains. The 'universal' and 'encyclopaedic' museums could be dissolved. There may be disagreements about some objects, such as the Elgin marbles, which have become national heritage in several countries. Other artefacts, with shared aesthetic and emotional appeal, may also remain contested. But numerous objects, many of which are not exhibited today and just fill up museum storage rooms, could be returned. Countless others, serving no other purpose than documenting the past, could simply be discarded. They would no longer be desired by anyone. Abandoning the things, however, would have downsides. Over the centuries, the passionate engagement with the past has opened new perspectives and possibilities. By amassing and exhibiting artefacts, scholars have encouraged the appreciation of

---

[127] Lowenthal, *Heritage Crusade*; Becker, *Yesterday*.   [128] Reinders, 'Monkey Kings'.

other values and viewpoints. The uncovering of historical differences has challenged authorities and questioned conventions. Still today, the encounter offers people, all over the world, opportunities to reconsider who they are and who they want to be. I doubt that an alternative world, without the things of the past, would be a better place to live.

Bibliography

Archival Material

British Museum, United Kingdom (BM)
 - Central Archive (CA)
Det Kongelige Bibliotek, Denmark (KB)
Museo Nacional de Colombia (MN)
Royal Anthropological Institute, United Kingdom (RAI)

Literature

Acosta, J. d. *Historia natural y moral de las Indias* (Sevilla: Juan de Leon, 1590).

Alexander, J. E. 'Notice of a Visit to the Cavern Temples of Adjunta in East-India', *Transactions of the Royal Asiatic Society*, 2 (1830), 362–70.

Allan, J. R. *Taipei* (Seattle, WA: University of Washington Press, 2012).

Ankermann, B. *Anleitung zum ethnologischen Beobachten und Sammeln* (Berlin: Reimer, 1914).

Ankermann, B. 'Kulturkreise und Kulturschichten in Africa', *Zeitschrift für Ethnologie*, 37 (1905), 54–90.

Arango, L. M. *Catálogo del museo del Sr. Leocadio María Arango* (Medellín: Imprenta Oficial, 1905).

Bacquart, J.-B. *The Tribal Arts of Africa* (London: Thames & Hudson, 1998).

Bastian, A. 'Bedeutung amerikanischer Sammlungen', *Zeitschrift für Ethnologie*, 21 (1889), 98–105.

Bastian, A. *Beiträge zur Ethnologie und darauf begründete Studien* (Berlin: Wiegandt und Hempel, 1871).

Bastian, A. *Die Culturländer des Alten America*, 3 vols. (Berlin: Weidmannsche Buchhandlung, 1878–89).

Bastian, A. *Die Heilige Sage der Polynesier* (Leipzig: Brockhaus, 1881).

Becerra, R. 'Circular á los Gobiernos de los Estados', *Anales de la Instuccion Pública en los Estados Unidos de Colombia*, 3 (September 1881), 11–2.

Becker, T. *Yesterday* (Cambridge, MA: Harvard University Press, 2023).

Biro, Y. *Fabriquer le regard* (Dijon: Les presses du réel, 2018).

Blier, S. P. *The History of African Art* (London: Thames & Hudson, 2023).

Boas, F. 'Some Principles of Museum Administration', *Science*, 25 (1907), 921–33.

Bodenstein, F. 'Die Diplomatie der Zurückweisung' in B. Savoy, R. Skwirblies, and I. Dolezalek (eds.), *Beute* (Berlin: Matthes & Seitz, 2021), pp. 348–54.

Bodenstein, F. 'Notes for a Long-Term Approach to the Price History of Brass and Ivory Objects Taken from the Kingdom of Benin in 1897' in B. Savoy, C. Guichard, and C. Howard (eds.), *Acquiring Cultures* (Berlin: De Gruyter, 2018), pp. 267–88.

Bolingbroke, H. S. J. L. *Letters on the Study and Use of History* (London: Millar, 1752).

Boone, E. H. 'Mesoamerican History' in J. Rabasa, M. Sato, E. Tortarolo, and D. Woolf (eds.), *The Oxford History of Historical Writing*, 5 vols. (Oxford University Press, 2011–15), vol. III, pp. 575–99.

Borda, J. J., 'Un Museo', *El Album* 6 (Bogotá, 29 June, 1856), 46–7.

Botero, C. I. *El redescubrimiento del pasado prehispànico de Colombia* (Bogotá: Universidad de los Andes, 2006).

Bredekamp, H. 'Franz Kugler and the Concept of World Art History' in P. N. Miller (ed.), *Cultural Histories of the Material World* (Ann Arbor: University of Michigan Press, 2013), pp. 249–62.

Breunig, P. (ed.), *Nok* (Frankfurt am Main: Africa Magna, 2014).

Brisson, J. *Viajes por Colombia en los Anos 1891 a 1897* (Bogotá: Imprenta Nacional, 1899).

Bryant, J. (ed.), *Art and Design for All* (London: V&A, 2012).

Burke, P. 'History, Myth, and Fictions' in J. Rabasa, M. Sato, E. Tortarolo, and D. Woolf (eds.), *The Oxford History of Historical Writing*, 5 vols. (Oxford University Press, 2011–15), vol. III, pp. 261–81.

Burke, P. *The Renaissance Sense of the Past* (London: Edward Arnold, 1969).

Cabello Carro, P. *Coleccionismo americano indigna en la España del siglo XVIII* (Madrid: Ediciones de Cultura Hispánica, 1989).

Cabello Carro, P. (ed.), *Política de la época de Carlos II en el área maya* (Madrid: Ediciones de la Torra, 1992).

Caicedo Rojas, J. *Informe del Conservador del Museo* (Bogotá, 20 October, 1881).

Cañizares-Esguerra, J. *How to Write the History of the New World* (Stanford: Stanford University Press, 2001).

Casaubon, M. *A Treatise of Use and Custome* (London: I. L., 1638).

Certeau, M. d. 'Writing vs. Time', *Yale French Studies*, 59 (1980), 37–54.

Cervantes, F. *The Devil in the New World* (New Haven, CT: Yale University Press, 1994).

Charpy, M. 'Trading Places' in B. Savoy, C. Guichard, and C. Howard (eds.), *Acquiring Cultures* (Berlin: De Gruyter, 2018), pp. 71–99.

Chakrabarty, D. *Provincializing Europe* (Princeton: Princeton University Press, 2008).

Cole, H. M. and Aniakor, C. C. (eds.), *Igbo Arts* (Los Angeles, CA: Museum of Cultural History, 1984).

Cuno, J. *Who Owns Antiquity* (Princeton: Princeton University Press, 2008).

Cuno, J. (ed.), *Whose Culture?* (Princeton: Princeton University Press, 2012).

Dagen, P. (ed.), *Charles Ratton* (Paris: Musée du quai Branly, 2013).

Earle, R. 'Monumentos y museos' in B. González-Stephan and J. Andermann (eds.), *Galerias del progresso* (Rosario: Beatriz Viterbo, 2006), pp. 27–56.

Edwards, A. B. *A Thousand Miles up the Nile* (London: Longmans, Green, 1877).

Erasmus, H. J. *The Origins of Rome in Historiography from Petrach to Perizonius* (Assen: Van Gorcum, 1962).

Eskildsen, K. R. 'Inventing the Archive', *History of the Human Sciences*, 26 (2013), 8–24.

Eskildsen, K. R. 'The Language of Objects', *Isis*, 103 (2012), 24–53.

Eskildsen, K. R. *Modern Historiography in the Making* (London: Bloomsbury, 2022).

Eskildsen, K. R. 'Fälschung' in M. Krajewski, A. v. Schöning, and M. Wimmer (eds.), *Enzyklopädie der Genauigkeit* (Konstanz: Konstanz University Press, 2021), pp. 130–9.

Espagnat, P. d. *Souvenirs de la Nouvelle Granade* (Paris: Bibliothèque-Charpentier, 1901).

Eudel, P. *Le Truquage* (Paris: Libraire de la Société des Gens de Lettres, 1884).

Evans, R. T. *Romancing the Maya* (Austin, TX: University of Texas Press, 2004).

Evju, H. *Ancient Constitution and Modern Monarchy* (Brill: Leiden, 2019).

Eyo, E. 'A Threat to National Art Treasures' in Y. R. Isar (ed.), *The Challenge to Our Cultural Heritage* (Washington, DC: Smithsonian Institution Press, 1986), pp. 203–31.

Eyo, E. 'Different Methods of Museum Education' in *Meeting on the Role of Museums in Education and Cultural Action* (Paris: ICOM, 1969), pp. 32–36.

Eyo, E. *Guide to the Nigerian Museum, Lagos* (N.p, 1969).

Eyo, E. 'The Nigerian National Museum, Lagos', *Interlink*, 4 (1967), 2–7.

Eyo, E. 'Preservation of Works of Art and Handicraft' in *Colloquium on Negro Art*, 2 vols. (N. p.: Présence Africaine, 1968), vol. I, pp. 577–87.

Eyo, E. 'Primitivism and Other Misconceptions in African Art', *Munger Africana Library Notes*, 12 (1982), 3–27.

Eyo, E. *Two Thousand Years of Nigerian Art* (Lagos: Federal Department of Antiquities, 1977).

Eyo, E. and Willett, F. *Treasures of Ancient Nigeria* (Detroit: Detroit Institute of Art, 1980).

Fabian, J. *Time and the Other* (New York: Columbia University Press, 2014).

Fagg, W. 'Art without Age', *Corona*, 2 (1950), 24–26.

Fagg, W. 'The Long Farewell', *Survival International Review* (Spring 1976), 23–24.

Fagg, W. *Masques d'Afrique* (Genève: Fernand Nathan, 1980).

Fagg, W. *Miniature Wood Carvings of Africa* (New York: Adams & Dart, 1970).

Fagg, W. *Nigerian Art* (Nottingham: Nottingham University Gallery, 1964).

Fagg, W. *Nigerian Images* (London: Lund Humphries, 1963).

Fagg, W. *One Hundred Notes on Nigerian Art from Christie's Catalogues*, E. Bassani (ed.) (N.p.: Carlo Monzino, 1991).

Fagg, W. *Traditional Art from the Colonies* (London: His Majesty's Stationary Office, 1951).

Fagg, W. 'Tribal Sculpture in the British Colonies', *Journal of the Royal Society of Arts*, 99 (1951), 688–706.

Fagg, W. 'Tribality' in *Colloquium on Negro Art*, 2 vols. (N. p.: Présence Africaine, 1968), vol. I, pp. 107–19.

Fagg, W. 'Tribality and Post-Tribality in the African arts,' in *African Fine Art Then & Now* (London: African Fine Arts Gallery, n. d), unpag.

Fagg, W. *Tribes and Forms in African Art* (London: Methuen, 1965).

Fagg, W. and Plass, M. *African Sculpture* (London: Studio Vista, 1964).

Fasolt, C. *The Limits of History* (Chicago: University of Chicago Press, 2004).

Feest, C. 'The Collecting of American Indian Artifacts in Europe, 1493–1750' in K. O. Kuppermann (ed.), *America in the European Consciousness 1492–1750* (Chapel Hill, NC: University of North Carolina Press, 1995), pp. 324–60.

Fendt, A. 'Antikeverständnis und Präsentationskonzepte in Berliner Alten Museum in 19. Jahrhunderts' in C. Schreiter (ed.), *Gipsabgüsse und antike Skulpturen* (Berlin: Reimer, 2012), pp. 73–94.

Fenollosa, E. F. *Epochs of Chinese & Japanese Art*, 2 vols. (New York: Frederik A. Stokes, 1912).

Fischer, M. 'Adolf Bastian's Travels in the Americas (1875–1876)' in M. Fischer, P. Bolz, and S. Kamel (eds.), *Adolf Bastion and his Universal Archive of Humanity* (Hildesheim: Olms, 2007), pp. 191–206.

Flood, F. B. 'Idol-Breaking as Image-Making in the "Islamic State"', *Religion and Society*, 7 (2016), 116–38.

Franch, J. A. *Arqueólogos o Anticuarios* (Barcelona: Ediciones del Serbal, 1995).

Fraser, G. 'A New Insight on Nigerian Art', *The New York Times* (October 12, 1982), 70.
Friedrich, M. *Die Geburt des Archivs* (Munich: Oldenbourg, 2013).
Fritzsche, P. *Stranded in the Present* (Cambridge, MA: Harvard University Press, 2004).
Frobenius, L. *Und Afrika sprach*, 3 vols. (Berlin: Vita, 1912–3).
Frobenius, L. *Der Ursprung der afrikanischen Kulturen* (Berlin: Gebrüder Borntraeger, 1898).
Fuhrmann, O. and Mayor, E. *Voyage d'Exploration Scientifique en Colombie* (Neuchâtel: Attinger, 1914).
Garcilaso de la Vega, *Commentarios reales* (Lisbon: Pedro Crasbeeck, 1609).
Giraldo, E. '"A" de Alzate', in *Ensayos sobre arte contemporáneo en Colombia 2013–2014* (Bogotá: Ediciones Uniandes, 2015), pp. 71–108.
Gliozzi, G. *Adam et le Nouveau Monde*, A. Estéve and P. Gabellone (trans.) (Nïmes: Théérète, 2000).
Goguet, A.-Y. *De l'origine des loix, des arts et des sciences et de leurs progrès chez les anciens peubles*, 3 vols. (Paris: Desaint & Saillant, 1758).
Gräbner, F. 'Kulturkreise und Kulturschichten in Ozeanien', *Zeitschrift für Ethnologie*, 37 (1905), 28–53.
Grafton, A. *New Worlds, Ancient Texts* (Cambridge, MA: Harvard University Press, 1992).
Grafton, A. *What Was History* (Cambridge: Cambridge University Press, 2007).
Grau, D. *Under Discussion* (Los Angeles, CA: Getty Research Institute, 2021).
Griggs, T. 'Universal History from Counter-Reformation to the Enlightenment', *Modern Intellectual History*, 4 (2007), 219–47.
Grout, N. *Museum Correspondences*, unpublished Ph.D. thesis, University of Brighton (2022).
Harloe, K. *Winckelmann and the Invention of Antiquity* (Oxford: Oxford University Press, 2013).
Hartog, F. *Régimes d'historicité* (Paris: Seuil, 2003).
Haskell, F. *History and its Images* (New Haven, CT: Yale University Presss, 1993).
Hellmann, A. H. *The Making of Museums in Nigeria* (Lanham, MD: Lexington Book, 2023).
Hicks, D. *The Brutish Museums* (London: Pluto Press, 2020).
Hoffmann, B. *Das Museum als Tausch- und Handelsgegenstand* (Berlin: LIT, 2012).
Hoyes, S. 'El Museo de D. Leocadio', *Repertorio Histórico de la Academia Antioqueña de Historia*, 1 (1905), 164–182.

Huddleston, L. E. *The Origins of the American Indians* (Austin, TX: University of Texas Press, 1967).

Humboldt, W. v. *Gesammelte Schriften*, 17 vols. (Berlin: B. Behr, 1903–1936).

Jacknis, I. 'The Ethnographic Object and the Object of Ethnology in the Early Career of Franz Boas' in G. W. J. Stocking (ed.), *Volksgeist as Method and Ethics* (Madison, WI: University of Wisconsin Press, 1996), pp. 185–214.

Jacobs, J. M. *Plunder?* (London: Reaktion Books, 2024).

Jenkins, I. *Archaeologists & Aesthetes in the Sculpture Galleries of the British Museum, 1800–1939* (London: British Museum Press, 1992).

Julien, C. 'Inca Historical Forms' in J. Rabasa, M. Sato, E. Tortarolo, D. Woolf (eds.), *The Oxford History of Historical Writing*, 5 vols. (Oxford: Oxford University Press, 2011–15), vol. III, pp. 619–39.

Kasfir, S. L. 'One Tribe, One Style?', *History in Africa*, 11 (1984), 163–93.

Kidd, C. *British Identities before Nationalism* (Cambridge: Cambridge University Press, 1999).

Kjersmeier, C. *Centres de style de la sculpture nègre africaine*, 4 vols. (Copenhagen: Fischer, 1935–38).

Kley, E. J. v. 'Europe's "Discovery" of China and the Writing of World History', *The American Historical Review*, 76 (1971), 358–81.

Koselleck, R. *Vergangener Zukunft* (Frankfurt am Main: Suhrkamp, 1979).

Kroeber, A. L. and Kluckhorn, C. *Culture* (New York: Vintage Books, 1952).

Kubler, G. 'Vico's Idea of America' in T. F. Reese (ed.), *Studies in Ancient American and European Art* (New Haven, CT: Yale University Press), pp. 296–300.

Kugler, F. *Handbuch der Kunstgeschichte* (Stuttgart: Ebner & Seubert, 1842).

Kume, K. *The Iwakura Embassy 1871–1873*, G. Healey and C. Tsuzuki (eds.), M. Collcutt et al. (trans.) 5 vols. (Matsudo: Japan Documents, 2002).

Kuper, A. *The Museum of Other People* (London: Profile Books, 2023).

La Condamine, C. M. 'Mémoire sur quelques anciens monumens du Perou, du temps des Incas', *Histoire de l'Academie Royal des Sciences et Belles Lettres. Année MDCCXLVI* (Berlin, 1748), pp. 435–56.

Lafitau, J.-F. *Mœurs des sauvages ameriquains compares aux mœurs des premiers temps*, 2 vols. (Paris: Saugrain, 1724).

Langebaek Rueda, C. H. *Los herederos del pasado*, 2 vols. (Bogotá: Editiones Uniandes, 2009).

Lenain, T. *Art Forgery* (Reaktion Books: London, 2011).

'Ley 34 de 1881 (20 de Mayo)', in *Año de 1881*. Vol. XXXI of *Codificacion Nacional de las Leyes de Colombia desde el año de 1821* (Bogotá: Imprenta Nacional, 1950), pp. 48–49.

'Ley 48 de 1918 (Noviembre 20)', in *Acto Legislativo y Leyes expedidas por el Congreso Nacional en su legislature del año de 1918* (Bogotá: Imprenta Nacional, 1919), pp. 96–99.

'Ley 47 de 1920 (Octubre 30)', in *Leyes expedidas por el Congresso Nacional en su legislature de 1920* (Bogotá: Imprenta Nacional, 1940), pp. 55–58.

Longair S. and McAleer, J. (eds.). *Curating Empire* (Manchester: Manchester University Press, 2012).

López Lugo, I. D. 'Autentificar, falsificar y patrimonializar', *Perseitas*, 10 (2022), 191–215.

Lorenz, C., and Bevernage, B. (eds.). *Breaking up Time* (Göttingen: Vandenhoeck und Ruprecht, 2013).

Lowenthal, D. *The Heritage Crusade and the Spoils of History* (Cambridge: Cambridge University Press, 1998).

Lowenthal, D. *The Past Is a Foreign Country* (Cambridge: Cambridge University Press, 1985).

Lozar, M. and Petrella, S. (eds.), *La Plume et le calumet* (Paris: Classiques Garnier, 2019).

Lubbock, J. *Pre-historic Times* (London: Williams and Norgate, 1865).

MacCormack, S. *Religion in the Andes* (Princeton: Princeton University Press, 1991).

Mackenzie, J. *Museums and Empire* (Manchester: Manchester University Press, 2009).

Magalhães, A. M. 'Da diáspora africana no Museu Histórico Nacional', *Anais do Museu Paulista*, 30 (2022), 1–29.

Magalhães A. M. and Plazzi, S. 'Brasil decolonial', https://artsandculture.google.com/story/KgVRV6elZHh-dw?hl=pt-BR.

Magalhães A. M. and Plazzi, S. 'Maria Cambinda', *Exposviões* (December 1, 2019).https://exporvisoes.com/2019/12/01/maria-cambinda-uma-mascara-uma-boneca-uma-escultura/.

Malaquais, D., and Vincent, C. 'Three Takes and a Mask' in N. Edjabe (ed.), *FESTAC '77* (Cape Town: Chimurenga, 2019), pp. 53–59.

Marchand, S. 'The Dialectics of the Antiquities Rush' in A. Fennick and N. Lubtchansky (eds.), *Pour une histoire d'archéologie XVIII siècle – 1945* (Bordeaux: Ausonius Editions, 2015), pp. 191–206.

Marchand, S. *German Orientalism in the Age of Empire* (Cambridge: Cambridge University Press, 2009).

Marchand, S. 'Priests among the Pygmies', in H. G. Penny an M. Bunzl (eds.), *Worldly Provincialism* (Ann Arbor, MI: University of Michigan Press, 2003), pp. 283–316.

Matytsin, A. M. *The Specter of Skepticism in the Age of Enlightenment* (Baltimore, MD: Johns Hopkins University Press, 2016).

Mead, C. W., 'South America', *Anthropological Papers of the Museum of Natural History*, 2 (1909), 330–47.

Meek, R. L. *Social Science and the Ignoble Savage* (Cambridge: Cambridge University Press, 1976).

Meinecke, F. *Erlebtes 1862–1901* (Leipzig: Koehler & Amelang, 1941).

Merchan, R. M., 'Antiguedades Americanas', *El Seminario*, 1 (April 1, 1886), 3.

Merryman, J. H. 'Two Ways of Thinking about Cultural Property', *The American Journal of International Law*, 80 (1986), 831–53.

Messling, G. 'Die Ägyptische Abteilung im Neuen Museum zu Berlin', *Jahrbuch der Berliner Museen*, 39 (1997), 71–98.

Miller, E. *That Noble Cabinet* (London: Andre Deutsch, 1971).

Miller, P. N. *History and its Objects* (Ithaca, NY: Cornell University Press, 2017).

Miller, P. N. (ed.). *Momigliano and Antiquarianism* (Toronto: University of Toronto Press, 2007).

Mitter, P. *Much Maligned Monsters* (Oxford: Clarendon Press, 1977).

Momigliano, A. 'Ancient History and the Antiquarian', *Journal of the Warburg and Courtauld Institutes*, 13 (1950), 285–315.

Monroe, J. W. 'The Market as "Artist"', *Critical interventions*, 12 (2018), 52–70.

Monroe, J. W. *Metropolitan Fetish* (Ithaca, NY: Cornell University Press, 2019).

Moreno de Ángel, P. 'El "Papel Periódico Ilustrado" y sus creadores', *Revista Credencial Historia*, 75 (1996), 8–11.

Morrison, J. H. 'Early Tin Production and Nigerian Labour on the Jos Plateau 1906–1921', *Canadian Journal of African Studies*, 11 (1977), 205–16.

Morse, E. S. *Japan Day by Day*, 2 vols. (Boston, MA: Houghton Mifflin Company, 1917).

Müller, H. 'Die Sammlungskonzeption des Museums für Deutsche Volkskunde von der Gründung 1889 bis zum ersten Weltkrieg', *Jahrbuch der Berliner Museen*, 34 (1992), 185–94.

Murphy, D. *The First World Festival of Negro Art, Dakar 1966* (Liverpool: Liverpool University Press, 2016).

Nyerup, R. *Historisk-statistiske Skildring af Tilstanden I Danmark og Norge i ældre og nyere Tider*, vol. 4 (Copenhagen: Soldin, 1806).

Okakura, K. *The Awakening of Japan* (New York: The Century Co, 1904).

Okakura, K. *The Book of Tea* (London: Putnam's Sons, 1906).

Okakura, K. *The Ideals of the East with Special Reference to the Art of Japan*, new ed. (London: John Murray, 1905).

Ostenfeld-Suske, K. v. 'Writing Official History in Spain, c. 1474–1600' in J. Rabasa, M. Sato, E. Tortarolo, and D. Woolf (eds.), *The Oxford History of Historical Writing*, 5 vols. (Oxford: Oxford University Press, 2011–15), vol. III, pp. 428–48.

Paul, C. *The First Modern Museums of Art* (Los Angeles: Paul Getty Museum, 2012).

Penny, H. G. 'Bastian's Museum' in H. G. Penny and M. Bunzl (eds.), *Worldly Provincialism* (Ann Arbor, MI: University of Michigan Press, 2003), pp. 86–126.

Penny, H. G. *In Humboldt's Shadow* (Princeton: Princeton University Press, 2021).

Penny, H. G. *Objects of Culture and Ethnographic Museums in Imperial Germany* (Chapel Hill, NC: University of North Carolina Press, 2002).

Phillips, M. S. *On Historical Distance* (New Haven, CT: Yale University Press, 2013).

Phillips, B., *Loot* (London: Oneworld, 2021).

Piazzini, C. E. 'Guaqueros, anticuarios y letrados' in C. H. Langebaek and C. I. Botero (eds.) *Arqueología y etnología en Colombia* (Bogotá: Universidad de los Andes, 2009), pp. 49–78.

Plessen, M.-L. v. 'Art and Design for All' in J. Bryant (ed.), *Art and Design for All* (London: V&A, 2012), pp. 11–19.

Pocock, J. G. A. *Barbarism and Religion*, 4 vols. (Cambridge: Cambridge University Press, 1999–2005).

Polllini, J. 'Christian Destruction and Mutilation of the Parthenon', *Mitteilungen des Deutschen Archiiologischen Instituts. Athenische Abteilung*, 122 (2007), 207–28.

Pombo, F. *Breve Guia del Museo Nacional, 20 de Junio* (Bogotá: Imprenta de Colunje i Vallarino, 1881).

Pombo, F. *Nueva Guia Descriptiva del Museo Nacional de Bogota* (Bogotá: Imprenta de 'La Luz', 1886).

Pomian, K. *Le musée, une histoire mondiale*, 3 vols. (Paris: Gallimard, 2020–22).

Popkin, R. H. *Isaac La Peyrère (1596–1676)* (Leiden: Brill, 1987).

Price, S. *Paris Primitive* (Chicago: University of Chicago Press, 2007).

Probst, P. *What Is African Art?* (Chicago: University of Chicago Press, 2022).

Pulszky, F. 'On the Progress and Decay of Art; and on the Arrangement of a National Museum', *The Museum of Classical Antiquities*, 5 (March 1852), 1–15.

Rabasa, J. 'Alphabetical Writing in Mesoamerican Historiography' in J. Rabasa, M. Sato, E. Tortarolo, and D. Woolf (eds.), *The Oxford History of Historical Writing*, 5 vols. (Oxford: Oxford University Press, 2011–15), vol. III, pp. 600–18.

Raffles, T. S. *The History of Java*, 2 vols. (London: Black, Parbury, and Allan, 1817).

Ranke, L. v. *Aus Werk und Nachlass*, W. P. Fuchs and T. Schieder (eds.), 4 vols (Munich: Oldenbourg, 1964–1975).

Ratton, C. *Masques africains* (Paris: Librairie des arts décoratifs, 1931).

Reinders, E. 'Monkey Kings Make Havoc', *Religion*, 34 (2004), 191–209.

Reyes Gavilán, A. L. 'Entre curiosidades del progreso nacional y objects etnográficos', *Maguaré*, 31 (2017), 113–51.

Robertson, G. *Who Owns History* (London: Biteback, 2019).

Robertson, W. *The History of America*, 2 vols. (London: Strahan, 1777).

Rodríguez Prada, M. P. *Le Musée National de Colombie 1823–1830* (Paris: L'Harmattan, 2013).

Rodríguez Prada, M. P. 'Museos, naturalistas y colecciones', *Curaduría de Historia*, 15 (2019), 13–45.

Rossi, P. *The Dark Abyss of Time*, L. G. Cochrane (trans.) (Chicago: University of Chicago Press, 1984).

Roux, E. d. and Paringaux, R.-P. *Razzia sur l'art* (Paris: Fayard, 1999).

Rowley-Conwy, P. *From Genesis to Prehistory* (Oxford: Oxford University Press, 2007).

Rubiés, J.-P. 'Theology, Ethnography, and the Historicization of Idolatry', *Journal of the History of Ideas*, 67 (2006), 571–96.

Rycaut, P. 'The Translator to the Reader' in Garcilasso de la Vega, *The Royal Commentaries of Peru in Two Parts* (London: Flescher, 1688), unpag.

Sarr, F. and Savoy, B. *Restituer le patrimoine africain* (Paris: Philippe Rey/Seuil, 2018).

Saville, M. H. 'Fraudulent Blackware Pottery of Colombia', *Indian Notes*, 5 (1928), 144–54.

Savoy, B. *Afrikas Kampf um seine Kunst* (Munich: C. H. Beck, 2021).

Scheele, M. *Wissen und Glaube in der Geschichtswissenschaft* (Heidelberg: Carl Winters Universitätsbuchhandlung, 1930).

Schlözer, A. L. *Einleitung in die ganze Nordische Geschichte*. Vol XXXI of *Fortsetzung der Algemeinen Welthistorie* (Halle: Gebauer, 1771).

Schlözer, A. L. *Vorstellung seiner Universal-Historie*, 2 vols. (Göttingen: Dietrich, 1772–3).

Schnapp, A. 'Ancient Europe and Native Americans' in D. Bleichmar and P. C. Mancall (eds.), *Collecting across Cultures* (Philadelphia, PN: University of Pennsylvania Press, 2011), pp. 58–79.

Schnapp, A. *La conquête du passé* (Paris: Carré, 1993).

Schnapp, A. *Une histoire universelle des ruines* (Paris: Seuil, 2020).

Schnapp, A. (ed.), *World Antiquarianism* (Los Angeles, CA: Getty Research Institute, 2013).

Scholder, K. *Ursprünge und Probleme der Bibelkritik im 17. Jahrhundert* (Munich: Chr. Kaiser, 1966).

Sheehan, J. *The Enlightenment Bible* (Princeton: Princeton University Press, 2005).

Steiner, C. B. *African art in transit* (Cambridge: Cambridge University Press, 1994).

Steinhauer, C. L. *Kort Veiledning i den nu ordnede Deel af det nye Ethnographiske Museum* (Copenhagen: Bianco Luno, 1849).

Storm, J. A. J. 'Excavating the Hall of Dreams', *Religions*, 13 (2022), 1–21.

Schwab, M. E. and Grafton, A. *The Art of Discovery* (Princeton: Princeton University Press, 2022).

Suzuki, H. *Antiquarians in Nineteenth-Century Japan*, M. Fukuoka (ed. and trans.) (Los Angeles, CA: Getty Research Institute, 2022).

Sydow, E. v. *Handbuch der Westafrikanischen Plastik* (Berlin: Dietrich Reimer / Ernst Vohsen, 1930).

Sweet, B. *Antiquaries* (London: Hambledon, 2004).

Tanaka, S. *Japan's Orient* (Berkely, CA: University of California Press, 1995).

Tanaka, S. *New Times in Modern Japan* (Princeton: Princeton University Press, 2004).

Thibault, C. *The Tribal Art Market 2000–2015* (N.p: Artkhade, 2015).

Thomsen, C. J. 'Kortfattet Udsigt over Mindesmærker og Oldsager fra Nordens Fortid' in *Ledetraad til nordisk Oldkyndighed* (Copenhagen: Møller, 1836), pp. 27–90.

Thomsen, C. J. *Kort Udsigt over det Kongelige Kunstmusæums forskjellige Afdelinger 1844* (Copenhagen: Bianco Luno, 1844).

Trigger, B. G. *A History of Archaeological Thought*, 2nd edn. (Cambridge: Cambridge University Press, 2006).

Tseng, A. Y. *The Imperial Museums of the Meiji Period* (Seattle, WA: University of Washington Press, 2008).

Uhle, M. *Kultur und Industrie südamerikanischer Völker*, 2 vols. (Berlin: Asher, 1889–90).

Vélez Vélez, L. F. 'Apuntes anecdoticos para la historia de la Ceramica Alzate' in *Colección Ceramica Alzate* (Medellín: Universidad de Antioquia, 1988), pp. 5–25.

Vierneisel, K. and Leinz, G. (eds.), *Glypthothek München 1830–1980* (Munich: Glyptothek, 1980).

Virchow, R. 'Verwaltungsbericht für das Jahr 1889', *Zeitschrift für Ethnologie*, 21 (1889), 725–34.

Völkel, M. 'German Historical Writing from the Reformation to the Enlightenment' in J. Rabasa, M. Sato, E. Tortarolo, and D. Woolf (eds.), *The Oxford History of Historical Writing*, 5 vols. (Oxford: Oxford University Press, 2011–15), vol. III, pp. 324–46.

Waterfield, H. 'Working with William', *African Arts*, 27 (1994), 30–31.

Weinstein, L. 'The Yumedono Kannon', *Archives of Asian Art*, 42 (1989), 25–48.

Weiss, R. *The Renaissance Discovery of Classical Antiquity* (Oxford: Basil Blackwell, 1959).

Weitmann, P. *Klassische Antike in den Berliner Museen 1797–1930* (Frankfurt am Main: Peter Lang, 2011).

Weston, V. *Japanese Painting and National Identity* (Ann Arbor, MI: University of Michigan Press, 2004).

Wimmer, M. *Archivkörper* (Konstanz: Konstanz University Press, 2012).

Woolf, D. R. *The Idea of History in Early Stuart England* (Toronto: University of Toronto Press, 1990).

Zedelmaier, H. *Der Anfang der Geschichte* (Hamburg: Meiner, 2003).

Zerda, L. *El Dorado* (Bogotá: Imprenta de Silvestre 1883).

Zerda, L. *El Dorado*, 2 vols. (Bogotá: Banco Popular, 1972).

Acknowledgements

The Carlsberg Foundation generously supported the research for this Element. It also benefitted from a visiting fellowship from the Vossius Center for the History of Humanities and Sciences, University of Amsterdam, and visits to Academia Sinica, Taipei, and University of the Andes, Bogotá. María José Montoya Durana helped navigate archives and libraries in Colombia. Suzanne Marchand, Carl Henrik Langebaek Rueda, Michael Harbsmeier, Jane Kim, Tom Foran, and colleagues at Roskilde University commented on earlier versions. The series editor, Daniel Woolf, and reviewers, Peter N. Miller, Thomas Stammers, and an anonymous reviewer, offered helpful suggestions to the book proposal and manuscript. Finally, I thank my wife Evelyn and my daughter Helena for support and tolerance.

Cambridge Elements

Historical Theory and Practice

Daniel Woolf
Queen's University, Ontario

Daniel Woolf is Professor of History at Queen's University, where he served for ten years as Principal and Vice-Chancellor, and has held academic appointments at a number of Canadian universities. He is the author or editor of several books and articles on the history of historical thought and writing, and on early modern British intellectual history, including most recently *A Concise History of History* (CUP 2019). He is a Fellow of the Royal Historical Society, the Royal Society of Canada, and the Society of Antiquaries of London. He is married with three adult children.

Editorial Board

Dipesh Chakrabarty, *University of Chicago*
Marnie Hughes-Warrington, *University of South Australia*
Ludmilla Jordanova, *University of Durham*
Angela McCarthy, *University of Otago*
María Inés Mudrovcic, *Universidad Nacional de Comahue*
Herman Paul, *Leiden University*
Stefan Tanaka, *University of California, San Diego*
Richard Ashby Wilson, *University of Connecticut*

About the Series

Cambridge Elements in Historical Theory and Practice is a series intended for a wide range of students, scholars, and others whose interests involve engagement with the past. Topics include the theoretical, ethical, and philosophical issues involved in doing history, the interconnections between history and other disciplines and questions of method, and the application of historical knowledge to contemporary global and social issues such as climate change, reconciliation and justice, heritage, and identity politics.

Cambridge Elements

Historical Theory and Practice

Elements in the Series

The History of Knowledge
Johan Östling and David Larsson Heidenblad

Conceptualizing the History of the Present Time
María Inés Mudrovcic

Writing the History of the African Diaspora
Toyin Falola

Dealing with Dark Pasts: A European History of Auto-Critical Memory in Global Perspective
Itay Lotem

A Human Rights View of the Past
Antoon De Baets

Historians' Autobiographies as Historiographical Inquiry: A Global Perspective
Jaume Aurell

Historiographic Reasoning
Aviezer Tucker

Pragmatism and Historical Representation
Serge Grigoriev

History and Hermeneutics
Paul Fairfield

Testimony and Historical Knowledge Authority, Evidence and Ethics in Historiography
Jonas Ahlskog

Race, Genetics, History New Practices, New Approaches
Alexandra P. Alberda, Njabulo Chipangura, Lara Choksey, Jerome de Groot, Maya Sharma

Things of the Past: A Modern Yearning
Kasper Risbjerg Eskildsen

A full series listing is available at: www.cambridge.org/EHTP

For EU product safety concerns, contact us at Calle de José Abascal, 56–1°, 28003 Madrid, Spain or eugpsr@cambridge.org.

www.ingramcontent.com/pod-product-compliance
Lightning Source LLC
LaVergne TN
LVHW011852060526
838200LV00054B/4285